Langenscheidt

The Zodiac Murders
Die Tierkreis-Morde

von Carole Eilertson
und Dagmar Puchalla

Langenscheidt

Berlin · München · Wien · Zürich · New York

Übungen von Carole Eilertson
Muttersprachliche Durchsicht: Charlotte Collins
Lektorat: Momo Evers
Coverfoto: Nancy Glor

Umwelthinweis: Gedruckt auf chlorfrei gebleichtem Papier

www.langenscheidt.de

ISBN-13: 978-3-468-44102-8
ISBN-10: 3-468-44102-9

One

Der Septemberabend in Hamburg war kalt und stürmisch. Laura eilte durch die hell erleuchtete Innenstadt und zog ihren neuen Ledermantel noch enger um den schmalen Körper. Aber es dauerte nicht mehr lange und sie hatte ihr Ziel erreicht.

Oh no, I'm late. The party's already started!

Neugierig schaute sie durch die riesigen Fenster in ein großes, festlich geschmücktes Buchgeschäft. Die Wände waren in einem warmen Orange gestrichen und einige der Bücherregale ragten in den Raum hinein. Trotzdem wirkte es weitläufig.

Viele Gäste waren bereits da, nippten an Champagnergläsern oder kosteten mit spitzen Lippen kleine Häppchen von silbernen Tabletts. Laura kannte niemanden von ihnen und verzog missmutig das Gesicht. Eine Partygängerin war sie noch nie gewesen, aber eine Party mit lauter wildfremden Menschen war das Schlimmste. Wo war nur Onkel Wolfgang?

I don't think I'll recognize him any more. He certainly won't recognize me after all these years.

Laura überlegte, kehrtzumachen und nach Hause zu fahren. Aber sie hatte Wolfgang versprochen, dass sie auch wirklich kommen würde.

Sie warf einen Blick auf ihr Spiegelbild im Fenster und ordnete mit wenigen Handgriffen ihr Haar neu. Sie sah gut aus, das wusste sie, weil man es ihr schon oft gesagt hatte. Dennoch gefiel sie sich selbst meist gar nicht. Jetzt zum Beispiel fand sie sich völlig unpassend angezogen und hoffnungslos unfrisiert. Dass sie aufgeregt war, machte die Sache nicht besser.

Sie beobachtete die Gäste in dem Laden. Onkel Wolfgang lebte schon seit langem in Amerika, war aber gerade mit seiner Frau von New York hierher gezogen. Laura wunderte sich, dass er trotzdem so viele Kontakte hatte.
So many people have come to the opening of his bookshop! It's ***incredible***.
Ihre Mutter war Engländerin gewesen, und auch wenn Laura sich kaum an sie erinnern konnte, war die englische Sprache stets wie ein Stück Heimat für sie gewesen. Sie war zweisprachig aufgewachsen, zumindest bis sie zu ihrer Großmutter gezogen und ihr Vater gestorben war. Ob sie Englisch oder Deutsch dachte oder sprach, fiel ihr bis heute meist gar nicht auf. Wenn sie von einem Buch erzählte und man sie fragte, in welcher Sprache sie es gelesen hatte, musste sie erst nachschauen. Jüngst hatte sie zudem fast ein Jahr lang in Kanada gearbeitet, aber vor einem Monat war ihre Großmutter gestorben und sie war zur Beerdigung nach Hamburg zurückgekehrt und geblieben.
'Uncle Wolfgang' war der beste Freund ihres vor Jahren verstorbenen Vaters gewesen. Aber sie hatte ihn als Kind schon sehr gemocht und immer Uncle zu ihm gesagt.
Irgendwann war er dann nach Amerika ausgewandert. Seit Großmutter nicht mehr lebte, war Wolfgang der einzige 'Verwandte', der Laura geblieben war. Alle anderen waren tot.
Sie seufzte, öffnete ihre Handtasche und wühlte darin herum. Ein runder Kompass fiel heraus und landete mit leisem Scheppern auf dem Gehsteig. Es war ein Lo-Pan Compass, ein Geschenk ihres Lehrers und eines ihrer wichtigsten Arbeitsutensilien als Innenarchitektin und Feng-Shui-Beraterin.

---

incredible [ɪnˈkredəbl] unglaublich

Als sie den Kompass aufhob, stellte sie erleichtert fest, dass er heil geblieben war. Liebevoll strich sie mit der Hand über ihn und steckte ihn in die Tasche zurück.
At least my compass isn't broken! But it looks ***as though*** *I've forgotten my business cards.* Genervt über sich selbst, rollte sie mit den Augen und betrachtete dann den eleganten Schriftzug über dem Eingang des Ladens:

Wolfgang Kaden
Englischsprachige Bücher – Seltene Bücher – Antiquariat

Und auf einem kleinen Schild in der Tür stand in verschnörkelter Schrift: 'Heute geschlossene Gesellschaft.'
Laura atmete ein letztes Mal tief durch, griff nach der schlichten, aber schweren schmiedeeisernen Klinke und öffnete die Tür.

Übung 1: Stimmen die folgenden Aussagen? Markieren Sie sie mit richtig (✓) oder falsch (×).

1. ☐ Laura wasn't late for the party.
2. ☐ Laura hasn't seen Wolfgang for many years.
3. ☐ Laura is Wolfgang's **niece**.
4. ☐ Wolfgang is a successful baker.
5. ☐ Laura received a compass from her teacher.
6. ☐ Laura loves parties.
7. ☐ Laura was living in Canada before her grandmother died.
8. ☐ Laura didn't want to go into the shop at first.

---

as though [əz 'ðəʊ] als ob **niece** [niːs] Nichte

Drinnen war es angenehm warm, und es duftete herrlich nach frischem Gebäck und exotischen Früchten. Unsicher mischte sich Laura unter die Gäste.

Ein Mann um die fünfzig mit stattlichem Bauch, freundlichem Lächeln und einem gut gefüllten Champagnerglas schaute neugierig zu ihr herüber und kam dann auf sie zu.

"Kann ich Ihnen behilflich sein?"

"Hm, ich weiß nicht . . . Mein Name ist Laura Krüger . . ."

Weiter kam sie nicht, denn der Mann unterbrach sie und rief über die Köpfe der Gäste hinweg. "Milena, Milena! Where are you? Come over here! Laura's finally arrived!"

Dann streckte er seine Arme aus und drückte die verdutzte Laura an sich.

Laura war das fürchterlich unangenehm; außerdem ging ihr das Ganze viel zu schnell. Aber sie versuchte, sich irgendwie zu entspannen, denn dieser Mann war vermutlich Onkel Wolfgang, auch wenn er sich in den vergangenen sechzehn Jahren wahrhaftig sehr verändert und Laura ihn als sportlichen, jungen Mann in Erinnerung hatte.

Eine elegante Frau, nicht viel älter als Laura, löste sich aus einer Gruppe exquisit gekleideter Damen, trippelte hüftenschwingend auf sie zu, hakte sich bei Wolfgang ein und lehnte ihren dunklen Pagenkopf an seine Schulter. Der Kontrast zwischen der fragilen, attraktiven Frau und ihrem sympathischen, aber massigen und auch schon betagteren Onkel erstaunte Laura. Wolfgang schien ihre Irritation nicht zu spüren, oder er ging generös darüber hinweg.

"Laura, ich freue mich sehr, dich zu sehen!" Sein Deutsch hatte einen leichten amerikanischen Akzent angenommen. "Actually, Laura, do you mind if we speak English?"

Laura lächelte. Tatsächlich hatte sie ihm auf seine Karten oft auf Deutsch geantwortet. 'Damit du die Sprache nicht verlernst', hatte sie ihm geschrieben. Irgendwann aber hatten sie einander immer seltener geschrieben. Traurig stellte Laura fest, dass sie mittlerweile nur noch sträflich wenig von dem Leben des jeweils anderen wussten. "No, not at all", sagte sie.

Wolfgang zwinkerte ihr zu. "Great! It's **a shame** you couldn't make it to the wedding, Laura. May I introduce you to my wife, Milena? She's a **native** New Yorker, and as she's only been in Hamburg for a week, her German isn't quite perfect yet . . ."

"Not quite perfect! Wolfie **is exaggerating**! My German is bad!" Milena hatte ein angenehmes, perlendes Lachen. "It's great to finally meet you **in person**, Laura. Wolfgang told me you're an interior designer. I'd love to get your opinion of our bookshop."

Laura nickte und sah sich um. Alles wirkte nobel und kostspielig, aber trotzdem gemütlich. Im Raum verteilt luden einzelne Sessel und kleine Beistelltischchen zum Sitzen und Lesen ein. Schräg in einer Ecke, nah beim Fenster, stand ein antiker Schreibtisch mit einem Computer darauf. Daran saß ein vertrauenerweckender älterer Herr, der gerade für einen Gast etwas ausdruckte. Laura vermutete, dass er ein Mitarbeiter von Wolfgang war. Sie lächelte verstohlen, ihr gefiel es hier von Augenblick zu Augenblick besser.

"Well, in my professional opinion, it looks . . . great!"

Wolfgang freute sich offensichtlich genauso wie seine Frau über Lauras Kompliment. Milena hatte ihm sicherlich beim Gestalten des Ladens geholfen.

"Milena comes from an old Italian family in New York. It

---

a shame [ə 'ʃeɪm] schade **native** ['neɪtɪv] gebürtig **to exaggerate** [ɪg'zædʒəreɪt] übertreiben **in person** [ɪn 'pɜːsn] persönlich didn't take much convincing to get her to come to Europe with me. **After all**, Hamburg is that much **closer** to Italy!"

Die beiden lachten ausgelassen, und Laura fühlte sich plötzlich ausgeschlossen.

Wolfgang streckte seine Hand aus und sah Laura auffordernd an. "Let me take your coat and your handbag! Help yourself to champagne and **canapés**!"

Als sie ihm ihre Handtasche überreichte, fiel erneut der Lo-Pan-Kompass heraus. Ehe Laura reagieren konnte, fing Milena ihn geschickt auf und betrachtete ihn neugierig, dann schob sie den Kompass vorsichtig zurück in Lauras Tasche.

Laura wurde für einen Moment unsicher. Laut aber sagte sie: "I'm so happy to see you again, Uncle Wolfgang. And I'm **delighted** to meet you, Milena. I **guess** you're all the family I have **left** now. Thanks for the wedding invitation. I'm so sorry I couldn't come but my grandmother died recently, and I just couldn't make it."

Milena nickte. "I know, *carina*. I'm so sorry . . ."

Es klang aufrichtig, und Laura fasste langsam etwas mehr Zutrauen zu der ihr fremden Frau. "My grandmother **brought** me **up**, you know."

"Oh, I see!", wisperte sie mitfühlend. "Poor Laura!"

Laura hatte plötzlich einen Kloß im Hals. Eigentlich waren beide, war selbst Wolfgang ein Fremder für sie. Sie ärgerte sich, dass sie ihre Großmutter überhaupt erwähnt hatte.

"But from now on we're your new family", rief Milena

---

after all [ˌɑːftər ˈɔːl] schließlich **closer** [ˈkləʊsə] näher **canapé** [ˈkænəpeɪ] Cocktailhäppchen **delighted** [dɪˈlaɪtɪd] entzückt **to guess** [ges] vermuten **left** [left] übrig **to bring (brought, brought) sb. up** [ˌbrɪŋ / ˌbrɔːt / ˌbrɔːt / ˈʌp] jmdn. großziehen

plötzlich begeistert aus, "I suppose I'm officially your aunt, aren't I?"
Einige der umstehenden Gäste unterbrachen ihr Gespräch und sahen zu ihnen herüber. Laura wäre am liebsten im Erdboden versunken, aber Milena hatte es schließlich nicht böse gemeint mit ihrer lautstarken Verkündung. Das war vermutlich nur ihr italienisches Temperament.
Als hätte sie Lauras Unwohlsein bemerkt, fuhr Milena leiser fort: "Well, let's be friends. Just call me Milena. 'Aunt Milena' makes me sound **ancient**!" Sie zwinkerte Laura verschwörerisch zu. "Anyway, Wolfgang isn't your real uncle."
"That's right", nickte Wolfgang. "But Laura's father Martin was my best friend, and you always called me 'uncle'. But when your mother . . . "
Er verstummte plötzlich und nahm einen viel zu großen Schluck von seinem Champagner.
Milena räusperte sich. "Perhaps we should change the **subject**, Wolfgang."
Am liebsten wäre Laura weggerannt, aber sie riss sich zusammen. "No, it's all right, Milena. After all, it's a long time ago. My mother died when I was two, my father when I was fourteen. He was a **sailor** and was always away on long sea **voyages**. I hardly ever saw him. My grandmother Eleanor brought me up practically **single-handedly**."
Milena wollte Lauras Hand nehmen, aber Laura mochte keine Sentimentalität.
Milena lachte leise. "There I go **putting** my **foot in** it again!

---

ancient [ˈeɪnʃənt] uralt **subject** [ˈsʌbdʒekt] Thema **sailor** [ˈseɪlə] Matrose **voyage** [ˈvɔɪɪdʒ] Reise **single-handedly** [ˌsɪŋglˈhændɪdlɪ] allein **to put (put, put) one's foot in sth.** [pʊt / pʊt / pʊt wʌnz ˈfʊt ɪn] ins Fettnäpfchen treten

Typical! Let's **grab** something to eat. The canapés are simply **divine**!"

Laura ließ sich von Milena zum Büffet ziehen, während Onkel Wolfgang ihre Sachen in einen Nebenraum brachte. Milena versuchte, das Gespräch auf etwas anderes zu lenken, und Laura war ihr mehr als dankbar dafür.
"Laura, what was that little thing in your handbag? That wooden thing with all those strange **engravings**."
"Oh that! It's a Lo-Pan compass. I've been doing a lot of feng shui with my clients recently. The compass is one of the most important **tools**.
Manchmal war Laura nicht sicher, ob Feng-Shui wirklich funktionierte, aber viele Leute waren begeistert, und schaden konnte es niemandem. Seitdem sie es zusätzlich zu ihrer Innenarchitektur anbot, hatte sie viele Kunden dazugewonnen.
Auch Milena schien von dem Thema begeistert zu sein. "How did you learn all about feng shui?"
"I went to Hong Kong to study it for three months, and I had a great mentor."
"And what do all the engravings on this Lopez compass mean?"
Für sie selbst völlig unerwartet musste Laura über die Namensverdrehung lachen. "It's called a Lo-Pan compass, not a Lopez compass. The engravings are quite **intriguing**, aren't they? They **represent** the twelve animals in the Chi-

---

typical [ˈtɪpɪkl] typisch **to grab** [græb] sich schnappen **divine** [dɪˈvaɪn] göttlich **engraving** [ɪnˈgreɪvɪŋ] Gravierung **tool** [tuːl] Werkzeug **intriguing** [ɪnˈtriːgɪŋ] faszinierend **to represent** [ˌreprɪˈzent] darstellen nese **Zodiac**. There's a **monkey**, a **rat and so on**. The Chinese **characters**[7] on the side mean, among other things, **wealth**, success, children and **loss**. Every area in your house **corresponds to** an area on the compass. I hope I'm not **getting** technical, but if you want to feel good, it's good to know where and how to start changing things at home – that is, of course, if you take feng shui seriously."

Milena war sichtlich begeistert. "Did you know that feng shui is **all the rage** in New York at the moment? I work for a **lifestyle** magazine – I've just taken a year's **sabbatical** to come and live in Hamburg. If you like, I can give you the phone number of our **editor**. You could write an article about feng shui for the magazine. New Yorkers really love that kind of thing." Dann verschwand ein köstliches Häppchen in ihrem Mund und sie verzog genießerisch das Gesicht.

In der Zwischenzeit war Wolfgang zurückgekehrt und lauschte dem Gespräch der beiden Frauen voller Interesse, ehe er noch einmal verschwand und einige Zeit darauf mit einem Berg von Leckereien auf seinem Teller zurückkam, was Milena natürlich nicht entging. "*Carino*," schimpfte sie scherzhaft, "what about your diet?"

"Next week, darling, next week! These canapés are delicious. In the words of Oscar Wilde, I can **resist** everything except **temptation**!"

---

zodiac ['zəʊdɪæk] Tierkreis(-zeichen) **monkey** ['mʌŋkɪ] Affe **rat** [ræt] Ratte **and so on** [ənd səʊ 'ɒn] und so weiter **character** ['kærəktə] *hier:* Schriftzeichen **wealth** [welθ] Reichtum **loss** [lɒs] Verlust **to correspond to sth.** [ˌkɒrə'spɒnd tə] etw. entsprechen **to get (got, got)** [get / gɒt / gɒt] *hier:* werden **all the rage** [ˌɔːl ðə 'reɪdʒ] der letzte Schrei **lifestyle** ['laɪfstaɪl] Lebensstil **sabbatical** [sə'bætɪkl] Ferienjahr **editor** ['edɪtə] Chefredakteur **to resist** [rɪ'zɪst] widerstehen **temptation** [temp'teɪʃn] Versuchung

Und dann schob sich das glückliche Paar mit viel Vergnügen gegenseitig Probierhäppchen in den Mund.
Laura biss in einen Cracker mit Avocadocreme und lächelte den beiden zu, auch wenn sie sich ziemlich fehl am Platz fühlte. Für einen schrecklichen Augenblick war ihr bewusst, wie einsam sie manchmal war.
"Isn't my wife **amazing**!", schwärmte Wolfgang erbarmungslos. "And according to feng shui I've already told everybody here tonight that a famous German feng shui **consultant** is **in our midst**. Tony Winkelmann, the **talk show host**, wants to meet you very much. Make sure you've got your business cards **handy**. That's him coming towards us now."
Laura spürte, wie sie errötete. "I'm afraid I've left my business cards at home."
"Well, here's a **pile** of **napkins**! These can be your business cards tonight. Just write your name and number on these!", schlug ihr Milena kichernd vor, und Laura lachte erleichtert mit. Ihre Unsicherheit verflog schlagartig, sie griff selbstbewusst nach den Servietten, als der Showmaster zu ihnen trat.
"Wolfgang, ist das hier die tolle Feng-Shui-Zauberin? Bitte stell uns vor. Ich muss nämlich mein Penthouse neu gestalten!"
Stolz legte Wolfgang seinen freien Arm um Lauras Schulter. "Allerdings, das ist sie!"
Dann flüsterte Onkel Wolfgang Laura ins Ohr: "Enjoy!

---

amazing [ə'meɪzɪŋ] erstaunlich **consultant** [kən'sʌltənt] Beraterin **in our midst** [ɪn aʊə 'mɪdst] (mitten) unter uns **talk show host** ['tɔːk ʃəʊ həʊst] Talkmaster **handy** ['hændɪ] zur Hand **pile** [paɪl] Stapel **napkin** ['næpkɪn] Serviette

But don't **sneak off** home without telling me. I've got something really important to show you later."

Übung 2: Wie lauten die besten Antworten auf die folgenden Aussagen?

1. My mother has just died.
2. I've just lost my job.
3. Help yourself to champagne.
4. Would you like some more canapés?
5. Your hair looks great!
6. Thanks for your help.
7. I'm going to Italy.
8. I'll give you a hand with your coat.

a. Have a nice trip!
b. I'm so sorry to hear that.
c. Thank you.
d. It's okay, thanks, I can manage.
e. Oh no! You poor thing!
f. Don't mention it! It was my pleasure.
g. I'm fine, thanks.
h. Thanks for the compliment.

Two

Es war bereits weit nach Mitternacht, als die Party sich dem Ende zuneigte.

"Hey, do you need any more napkins to write your name on?" Milena war neben Laura aufgetaucht und zwinkerte ihr zu. Diese war gerade dabei, ihre Telefonnummer und

---

to sneak off [ˌsniːk ˈɒf] sich davonschleichen

E-Mail-Adresse auf eine Serviette zu kritzeln. "I'll go and find Wolfgang and ask him to organize a few dozen more if you like."
Laura schüttelte den Kopf.
"It's been a huge success for you here this evening, hasn't it?", fragte Milena voller Freude.
"Yes. Thanks to you!", flüsterte Laura, während sie ihrem zukünftigen Kunden lächelnd die Serviette reichte. Er bedankte und verabschiedete sich.
Laura fühlte sich erstaunlich wohl in Milenas Nähe, so wohl wie selten. Ihre Freundinnen waren eigentlich alle eher gute Bekannte. Und einen Freund wollte Laura nicht. Keinen Mann, und erst recht keine Kinder. Dann konnte man alles andere gleich an den Nagel hängen; das sah sie bei einigen Kolleginnen, die versucht hatten, Familie und Karriere zu verbinden. Die waren alle vollkommen überlastet. Auch wenn die Medien immer kluge Ratschläge parat hatten, die Arbeit nahm einem keiner ab. Sie wollte frei und unabhängig sein, reisen, so oft und wohin sie wollte, und dabei viel, viel Geld verdienen.
Milena hakte sich bei ihr ein und zog sie in den hinteren Teil der Buchhandlung. "It looks like Wolfgang is saying goodbye to the last guests now. Let's go to his office and wait for him there."
Ein klein wenig beschwipst von Erfolg und Champagner folgte Laura ihr.

Wolfgangs Büro entsprach gar nicht Lauras Geschmack; es war vollgestopft mit Kisten, Büchern, Papieren und Manuskripten, die sich an allen nur erdenklichen Stellen zu Bergen türmten. Auf dem riesigen, übervollen Schreibtisch thronten ein Globus und, zu Lauras Überraschung,

verschiedene Ferngläser. Seufzend vor Erschöpfung ließ Milena sich auf ein großes Ledersofa fallen.
Dann wandte sie sich Milena zu.
"How did you two meet? Had you been going out for long before you decided to **take the plunge**?"
Ein geheimnisvolles Lächeln huschte über Milenas Gesicht, und seufzend rutschte sie ein bisschen tiefer in die Kissen des Sofas. "Ah, well, that's a long story. Several months ago Wolfgang was at a book fair in New York, and our magazine was supposed to write a piece on it. *The New York Book Fair* is a highlight of the year, and we wanted an interview with Wolfgang Kaden because he was one of the most successful European **dealers** in old manuscripts. Because my freelancer was sick, I had to do it myself."
Laura, die noch immer neben dem Schreibtisch stand und an ihrem Champagner nippte, wurde nachdenklich. "It seems I don't know much about Wolfgang at all. I never knew he was famous."
Milena lachte einmal mehr ihr angenehmes, perlendes Lachen. Für eine Frau hatte sie eine tiefe, aber warme Stimme, die einnehmend und beruhigend zugleich auf Laura wirkte.
"Well, I wouldn't say that he was famous. But he is well-known among book dealers. He's one of the leading experts on 17th century texts on medicine, **medicinal plants** and . . . birds!"
"He's never ever told me that!"

---

to take (took, taken) the plunge [ˌteɪk / ˌtʊk / ˌteɪkn ðə 'plʌndʒ] den Sprung wagen **dealer** ['diːlə] Händler **medicinal plant** [məˌdɪsnəl 'plɑːnt] Heilpflanze

"Well, he is quite a **modest** guy." In Milenas Worten schwang unüberhörbar der Stolz auf ihren Mann mit.

Übung 3: Milena interviewed Wolfgang in New York. Bitte setzen Sie die richtigen Formen des Past Simple ein.

Milena: How did you get interested in collecting books?

Wolfgang: As a child I often **1.** *(go)* went __________ bird-watching. I always **2.** *(have)* __________ a camera with me. Whenever I **3.** *(see)* __________ interesting birds, I **4.** *(take)* __________ photos of them and **5.** *(stick)* __________ them into my album. I **6.** *(know)* __________ most of the birds but still didn't recognize all of them. One day I **7.** *(buy)* __________ a book about birds in an old bookshop. I **8.** *(pay)* __________ very little money for it. I **9.** *(keep)* __________ it in my room. One day my father **10.** *(come)* __________ into my room and **11.** *(find)* __________ the book. He explained that the book **12.** *(be)* __________ very **rare** and **13.** *(be)* __________ **worth** a lot of money. That's how I **14.** *(become)* __________ interested in collecting books.

---

modest ['mɒdəst] bescheiden **rare** [reə] selten **worth** [wɜːθ] wert

In dem Moment betrat Wolfgang stöhnend den Raum.
“Tony Winkelmann **was** quite **taken with** you, Laura. But I fear he’s had one glass of champagne too many. I’ve just **sent** him **packing**! But my ears are burning! Modest? Who’s modest? Not me, surely!”
Laura grinste. “I just wanted to know how you two met . . .”
Wolfgang schlenderte um seinen Schreibtisch herum und ließ sich in den großen Sessel fallen. “It was a real **whirlwind romance**, wasn’t it, darling?” Er zwinkerte seiner Frau zu, doch dann wurde er ernst. “Laura, I wanted to see you again, of course, and I wanted you to meet Milena . . . but there’s another important reason why I wanted you here.”
Schlagartig hatte Laura das Gefühl, die ganze Atmosphäre im Raum würde sich verdichten. Auch Milena sah sie jetzt aufmerksam an. Lauras Herz raste, und plötzlich hatte sie Angst.
“Laura, as you know, I have no children of my own. I’ve always felt close to you, and I wish I**’d kept in touch** – but things got complicated . . .” Wolfgang hielt inne, zog aus einer Schublade eine Schatulle und stellte sie vor sich hin auf den Tisch.
“As you know, you were born in Cornwall . . .”, setzte er neu an.
Milena unterbrach ihn. “Where were you born exactly, Laura?”

---

to be (was, been) taken with sb. [biː / wɒz / biːn ˈteɪkən wɪð] von jmdm. angetan sein **to send (sent, sent) sb. packing** [send / sent / sent / ˈpækɪŋ] jmdn. fortjagen **whirlwind romance** [ˈwɜːlwɪnd rəʊˌmæns] stürmische Romanze **to keep (kept, kept) in touch** [ˌkiːp / ˌkept / ˌkept ɪn ˈtʌtʃ] in Kontakt bleiben

Laura wurde bleich. "I was born on a **remote** island off the coast of Cornwall. My mother's name was Bridget Pencoe and the island belonged to her. She died when I was two years old, and that's when I came to Hamburg. As far as I know, my mother's family had owned the island for generations. Some **ancestor** of mine helped one of the English kings in some **battle**, and the king gave him the island as a **reward**. But that's about all I know." Sie hatte das alles heruntergeleiert wie einen auswendig gelernten Text. Jetzt schwieg sie.
Wolfgang nahm den Faden wieder auf. "Martin and I met Bridget when we went to Cornwall on holiday. Martin wasn't interested in bird-watching like me, but he loved being outdoors. We met Bridget on Rose Island. You look a lot like her, Laura", fügte er leise hinzu. "Bridget was a great cook, and I think both Martin and I fell in love with her food." Offenbar wollte er einen Scherz machen, aber Laura spürte, dass da noch etwas anderes war.
"Well, Martin and Bridget fell in love. They got married shortly afterwards – this was all over thirty years ago – and two years later you were born. They called you Rhiannon. That's a **Celtic** name. Laura is actually your middle name, isn't it?"
Lauras Mund war so ausgetrocknet wie eine Wüstenlandschaft. "Oma didn't want to call me Rhiannon. She said it was too difficult to pronounce." Sie hätte jetzt gerne etwas getrunken, aber ihr Glas war leer. "I wish somebody had talked to me about my mother when I was **growing up**.

---

remote [rɪ'məʊt] abgelegen **ancestor** ['ænsestə] Vorfahr **battle** ['bætl] Schlacht **reward** [rɪ'wɔːd] Belohnung **Celtic** ['keltɪk] keltisch **to grow (grew, grown) up** [ˌgrəʊ / ˌgruː / ˌgrəʊn 'ʌp] aufwachsen

Oma always said '**Ignorance is bliss**'. I grew up believing that my mother must have done something . . .", Laura schluckte, ". . . something **dreadful**."
Laura schluckte erneut, um ihre Kehle anzufeuchten. Wollte sie wirklich mehr wissen? Genau das war der eigentliche Grund gewesen, weshalb sie in den letzten Jahren nie eine von Wolfgangs Einladungen nach Amerika angenommen hatte. Sie hatte den Moment, an dem sie die Wahrheit erfahren würde, sowohl herbeigesehnt als auch gefürchtet.
Wolfgang klang sehr traurig, als er fortfuhr. "I respected Eleanor – I mean your grandmother – a lot for bringing you up. But she wouldn't let anyone get close to you. I tried to get her to talk to you about Bridget, but she was very **stubborn**. She held your mother **responsible** for ruining Martin's life. But that's why I asked you here tonight, Laura. Your grandmother is dead now. **By the way**, I'm sorry I didn't make it to the funeral. It was on our wedding day, as you know. But Laura, I think the time has now come for you to learn the truth."
Laura war, als würde ihre Oma das Gespräch belauschen. Sie wollte nicht schlecht von ihr denken, schließlich hatte ihre Großmutter es immer gut mit ihr gemeint. Abrupt stand sie auf und lief hinaus in den großen, noch immer von sanftem Licht erleuchteten Raum. Am liebsten wäre sie weggerannt und nie wiedergekommen. Es war schön, dass die beiden da waren, aber mussten sie unaufhörlich über ihr, Lauras, Leben reden? Alle waren tot, es gab nichts zu reden und man

---

Ignorance is bliss. ['ɪgnərəns ɪz 'blɪs] Was ich nicht weiß, macht mich nicht heiß. **dreadful** ['dredfl] furchtbar **stubborn** ['stʌbən] dickköpfig **by the way** [baɪ ðə 'weɪ] übrigens konnte erst recht nichts daran ändern. Sollte sie einfach nach Hause gehen? Aber ... *was ignorance really bliss?*

Übung 4: Wie heißt das Gegenteil? Setzen Sie die richtigen Ziffern ein.

1. ignorance	☐	lie
2. warm	☐	close
3. remote	☐	hate
4. reward	☐	unhappy
5. stubborn	☐	easy-going
6. happy	☐	punishment
7. love	☐	cool
8. truth	☐	knowledge

Laura starrte in ihr leeres Glas. Nein, sie wollte es jetzt wissen. Entschlossen griff sie nach einer Flasche Champagner und zwei zusätzlichen Gläsern, dann kehrte sie zu Wolfgang und Milena zurück, die sie schweigend erwarteten. Während sie die drei Gläser fast bis zum Rand füllte und den beiden je eines reichte, sagte sie mit fester Stimme: "I loved Oma very much, but now that she's gone I want to know everything about my mother. Did she really **run off with** another man and **abandon** me, like Oma said?" Sie trank in einem Zug das Glas fast leer und wurde langsam wieder ruhiger. "I want to find out who I really am."
Anerkennend nickte Wolfgang ihr zu. "It's a long story. But **rest assured**, Laura, I'm sure your mother never did anything you should **be ashamed of**." Auch er nahm einen

---

to run (ran, run) off with sb. [ˌrʌn / ˌræn / ˌrʌn ˈɒf wɪð] mit jmdm. durchbrennen **to abandon** [əˈbændən] verlassen **rest assured** [rest əˈʃɔːd] verlass dich darauf **to be (was, been) ashamed of sth.** [biː / wɒz / biːn əˈʃeɪmd əf] sich schämen für etw.

großen Schluck Champagner und atmete tief durch, ehe er fortfuhr. "After Bridget and Martin got married, Bridget set up a kind of health and beauty **spa** on the island with her business partner, Sylvie Stone. Martin was often at sea, but he spent as much time as possible with you and Bridget. I visited them a couple of times. When you were about two years old, one morning in December, a few days before Christmas, something awful happened. Bridget got onto the boat to the **mainland** and never came back. Nobody ever saw her again. She simply **vanished into thin air**."

In Lauras Kopf rasten die Gedanken wie wild gewordene Vögel. "My Oma told me that she was either dead or had run off with some man!"

"I don't think she ran off with anybody. She loved you both too much for that. I think she must have had an accident. The police **investigated** her death but they never found any **clues**. Everyone **assumed** that she must have somehow fallen **overboard** – without anyone noticing. You see, no body was ever found. Ten years after she . . . vanished, she **was** officially **declared dead**. It's a mystery to this day, what happened to her."

Lauras Hände zitterten. Sie stellte das Champagnerglas auf den Schreibtisch und ließ sich neben Milena auf das Sofa sinken. "What did my father do?", flüsterte sie.

"You and Martin were waiting for Bridget to join you for

---

spa [spɑː] *hier:* Farm **mainland** [ˈmeɪnlənd] Festland **to vanish into thin air** [ˈvænɪʃ ɪntə ˌθɪn ˈeə] sich in Luft auflösen **to investigate** [ɪnˈvestɪgeɪt] untersuchen **clue** [kluː] Hinweis **to assume** [əˈsjuːm] annehmen **overboard** [ˈəʊvəbɔːd] über Bord **to be (was, been) declared dead** [biː / wɒz / biːn dɪˌkleəd ˈded] für tot erklärt werden

Christmas in Hamburg. But she never **turned up**. Martin almost went mad with worry. He flew over to Britain and went to the health spa on Rose Island to look for her. Several people saw her leave, but nobody knew where she went afterwards. Ten years after she died, Martin sold the spa and the island to Bridget's partners, Sylvie and Clive Stone. Then he spent the rest of his life **grieving** for Bridget."

Laura konnte keinen klaren Gedanken fassen. War alles, was sie bislang über ihre Eltern gedacht hatte, falsch gewesen?

Milena rückte näher an sie heran und legte den Arm um ihre Schulter. Die ungewohnte Nähe ließ Laura zusammenzucken, und Milena zog ihren Arm sofort zurück. "Sorry", wisperte sie kaum hörbar.

Laura schaute in Milenas Gesicht. Sie sah so besorgt aus. "It's okay, Milena. It's not as if I even have any **conscious** memories of my mother. I never think about her at all, except . . . "

"Except when?"

In ihrer Kehle zog sich alles zusammen, und nur zögernd fuhr Laura fort. "I sometimes have this dream – I had it last night too. I've had it all my life and it's nearly always the same. It's more of a **nightmare** really. I'm running along the top of a steep **cliff**. The sky is **crimson** – the colour of blood. There are some birds in the sky. Huge, black, **monstrous**-looking birds. I don't recognize the **coastline**. It's strange – very **rugged**. Down below on the beach I can just

---

to turn up [ˌtɜːn ˈʌp] auftauchen **to grieve** [griːv] trauern **conscious** [ˈkɒnʃəs] bewusst **nightmare** [ˈnaɪtmeə] Albtraum **cliff** [klɪf] Felsen **crimson** [ˈkrɪmzn] karmesinrot **monstrous** [ˈmɒnstrəs] monströs **coastline** [ˈkəʊstlaɪn] Küstenlinie **rugged** [ˈrʌgɪd] schroff about **make out** a few little **coves**. The sun is just **setting** in the west. All at once, I can hear footsteps behind me. I can feel hot breath on my neck. Someone's **chasing** me. I have to get away. I **keep on** running – faster and faster. Suddenly someone pushes me from behind. I **stumble**. Then I fall. I fall down and down, towards the black sea water below. I'm screaming **at the top of my voice**." Ihre Stimme war immer leiser geworden und nun kaum mehr als ein Flüstern. "I'm screaming – Mama."

Der Kloß in ihrem Hals war nun so groß, dass sie das Schluchzen nicht mehr unterdrücken konnte. Sie fühlte sich unendlich allein auf der Welt. Als Wolfgang aufsprang und sich vor sie hinkniete und er und seine Frau sie in die Arme nahmen, ließ sie es geschehen. Sie weinte so hemmungslos, wie sie nicht einmal am Grab ihrer Oma geweint hatte.

Übung 5: Bringen Sie die Ereignisse der Handlung in die richtige Reihenfolge.

1. ☐ Bridget mysteriously vanished on her way to Germany.
2. ☐ Martin fell in love with Bridget.
3. ☐ Laura was born.
4. ☐ Bridget was declared officially dead. Martin sold the spa and the island.
5. ☐ Martin and Wolfgang went on holiday to Cornwall.
6. ☐ Martin flew to Britain to search for his wife.

---

to make (made, made) out [ˌmeɪk / ˌmeɪd / ˌmeɪd ˈaʊt] erkennen **cove** [kəʊv] kleine Bucht **to set (set, set)** [set / set / set] untergehen **to chase** [tʃeɪs] jagen **to keep (kept, kept) on doing sth.** [ˌkiːp / ˌkept / ˌkept ɒn ˈduːɪŋ] etw. weiter machen **to stumble** [ˈstʌmbl] stolpern **at the top of my voice** [ət ðə ˈtɒp əv maɪ ˈvɔɪs] aus vollem Halse

7. ☐ Bridget set up a health spa on the island.
8. ☐ Martin took Laura to Hamburg to visit her grandmother.
9. ☐ Laura started to have nightmares.

Als sie wieder ruhiger geworden war, seufzte sie tief: “I’m sorry, I don’t know what you must think of me. I’ve usually got a bit more self-control.”
Milena schüttelte den Kopf. “Don’t worry, Laura. You’ve got every right to be **upset**.”
“Thank you so much . . .” Ihr Dank kam aus tiefstem Herzen. So durcheinander Laura war, so geborgen fühlte sie sich bei den beiden. Dann fiel ihr Blick auf die Schatulle. “That little box? What’s in there?”, wisperte sie.
“I don’t know, Laura. It’s yours.” Wolfgang stand auf und brachte sie ihr. “I’ve no idea what’s inside. I’ve never looked. Martin asked me to give it to you when Oma Eleanor died.”
Mit zitternden Händen öffnete Laura die Schatulle, die wie eine kleine Schatztruhe aussah.
Das erste, was Laura erblickte, war ein ausgerissener vergilbter Zeitungsartikel. Ihre Augen huschten darüber; dabei hielt sie das Blatt so, dass Wolfgang und Milena mitlesen konnten.

THE SCILLY **ISLES** GAZETTE, DECEMBER 31st 1975.
OWNER OF **CHIC** SPA VANISHES INTO THIN AIR.
Bridget Pencoe, the owner of the **Ruby** Rose Spa, has vanished into thin air. She left the island on 21st December, **intending** to fly from London to Hamburg to spend Christ-

---

upset [ˌʌp'set] durcheinander **isle** [aɪl] Insel **chic** [ʃiːk] schick
ruby ['ruːbɪ] Rubin **to intend** [ɪn'tend] vorhaben

mas with her husband and small daughter, Rhiannon. Several people saw her board the small ferry to St Mary's where Dr Clive Stone, Sylvie Stone's husband, dropped her off before returning to Rose Island. The police have interviewed several passengers on the Scillonian, the ferry service that connects St Mary's to Penzance on the mainland. Some passengers confirm that a tall **blonde** woman **matching** Bridget's description was on board the Scillonian that afternoon. Mysteriously, however, Mrs Pencoe never arrived in Germany.
Mrs Pencoe is in her late twenties. She has long blonde hair and green eyes. She is slim and about five feet ten inches tall.

Ein Schauder durchrieselte Lauras Körper. "Green eyes like me and blonde like me", flüsterte sie, und ihre Hände zitterten.

Mrs Pencoe **remodelled** her house two years ago **in order to** open a health and beauty spa with her partner, Mrs Sylvie Stone – **formally** Sylvie Barée, the famous star of the popular historical T.V. **drama series Hearts Asunder**.

"Does the spa still exist?", fragte Laura.

---

blonde [blɒnd] blond **to match** [mætʃ] entsprechen **to remodel** [ˌriːˈmɒdl] umbauen **in order to** [ɪn ˈɔːdə tə] um … zu **formally** [ˈfɔːməlɪ] geborene **drama series** [ˈdrɑːmə ˌsɪərɪːz] Dramaserie **'Hearts Asunder'** [ˌhɑːts əˈsʌndə] 'Herzen Auseinander' *(Eigenname)*

Wolfgang schaute etwas verlegen auf seine Hände. "Yes it does, and it's very successful."
Plötzlich war der Gedanke da. Laura wollte auf diese Insel, wollte sehen, wo sie geboren wurde, wollte alles wissen, was es dort über sie und ihre Mutter zu erfahren gab.
Und dann sah sie das Foto ihrer Mutter in der Schatulle. Es hing an einem kleinen Päckchen und erschien ihr unendlich vertraut. Ihre Mutter lächelte ihr aufmunternd zu.
Zaghaft lächelte Laura zurück, dann packte sie vorsichtig das kleine Päckchen aus.
"What is it?", fragte Milena, als ein kleines Püppchen zum Vorschein kam.
Wolfgang seufzte. "It's a small hand-knitted doll", erklärte er. "See her long white **costume** with its black and gold **edges**? That was the traditional **dress** of 19th century Cornish women. I think I even remember Bridget making this doll for you that Christmas – the year she disappeared. Look, there's your name knitted on the back."
Auf dem Kragen der zierlichen Puppe stand tatsächlich in Schnörkelschrift *Rhiannon.*
Laura starrte abwechselnd auf die Puppe und das Foto ihrer Mutter, die auf dem Bild nicht viel älter war als sie selbst jetzt. "It's exquisite. It must **have taken** her **ages** to make it." Ihr wurde warm ums Herz. Noch nie, so erschien es ihr, hatte ihr jemand etwas so Schönes geschenkt.
"What happened to Martin?", fragte Milena ihren Mann.
Wolfgang wollte ihr antworten, aber Laura war schneller.

---

costume [ˈkɒstjuːm] Tracht **edge** [edʒ] Saum **dress** [dres] *hier:* Kleidung **to take (took, taken) ages** [teɪk / tʊk / teɪkn ˈeɪdʒəs] eine Ewigkeit dauern

Übung 6: Setzen Sie die richtige Alternative ein.

"He **1.** .... *(quick/quickly)* became an alcoholic. Of course I didn't know that **2.** .... *(immediate/immediately)*. Whenever Oma told me that he was coming back from one of his voyages I got so **3.** .... *(excited/excitedly)* that I could **4.** .... *(hard/hardly)* sleep at night. I couldn't wait to see him. All the other girls in my class had **5.** .... *(perfect/perfectly)* **6.** .... *(normal/normally)* fathers, you know. The kind who didn't disappear for months on end on sea voyages." Laura machte eine kleine Pause und versuchte, sich an ihren Vater zu erinnern. "When his ship was coming in, Oma and I went down to the harbour as **7.** .... *(fast/quick)* as possible to meet him. It was so exciting! People from all over the world would be talking in different languages and walking around the docks. It was always easy to **spot** my father's ship. Its sides were huge – I felt as if I were standing in front of a **8.** .... *(steep/steeply)* white wall, watching **9.** .... ***(eager**/eagerly)* to see my father. When he finally got off

---

to spot [spɒt] entdecken **eager** ['iːgə] gespannt

the ship, he used to hold me in his arms and give me a big kiss." Laura atmete tief durch. Ihr war, als ob der Geruch ihres Vaters plötzlich im Raum schwebte. "I could smell something **10.** ________ ____________ *(terrible/terribly)* – something sour – on his breath. I didn't know until years later that it was alcohol."

Sie lächelte. Die Erinnerung hatte trotz allem auch etwas Tröstliches. "Being his daughter has actually given me a sort of advantage. Since I was a child I've always been sensitive to smells. Most other feng shui consultants don't pay enough attention to smells. But I pay attention to all the senses – touch, smell and taste as well as **sight** and **hearing** . . ."

Laura hielt inne und schaute in Wolfgangs offenes, abwartendes Gesicht. Und auf einmal erinnerte sie sich an seine Augen, als sie noch ein kleines Kind gewesen war und er sie hochgehoben hatte, an diese Augenblicke kindlicher Unschuld und Freude, die sie mit ihm vor langer Zeit geteilt hatte. "Uncle Wolfgang, I want to find out what happened to Bridget. I need to know the truth."

Wolfgang nickte zögernd. "Okay, but it's not going to be easy. Bridget disappeared almost twenty-eight years ago. Your father **left no stone unturned**. Even the police finally gave up."

Aber Lauras Entschluss war gefasst. "I grew up believing

---

sight [saɪt] Sehen **hearing** [ˈhɪərɪŋ] Hören **to leave (left, left) no stone unturned** [ˈliːv / ˈleft / ˈleft nəʊ ˌstəʊn ʌnˈtɜːnd] nichts unversucht lassen that my mother had died. But maybe she's still alive somewhere ... "

Abrupt drehte Wolfgang sich um und ging hinter seinen Schreibtisch. "I don't think she's alive, Laura. Otherwise I'm sure she would have been in touch with you or Martin. I don't want you to have any false hopes."

Lauras Hoffnung zerbrach in tausend Stücke, und der Kloß kehrte in ihre Kehle zurück. Dennoch konnte sie nichts mehr zurückhalten. "**My mind's made up!** I have to get to this island as soon as possible."

Wolfgang versuchte, sie zu bremsen. "Sleep on it, Laura. There are no guarantees that you'll find anything out. And sometimes playing detective can be ... dangerous."

Milena sah ihn überrascht an. "Now calm down, Wolfie. It's up to her to decide what she wants to do with her life. I don't know why you're getting upset."

"It's okay, Milena", beschwichtigte Laura sie. "I know Wolfgang is trying to protect me. Oma tried to protect me too. But you're right. I can make my own mind up. I have to find out the truth."

Ohne ein weiteres Wort zog Wolfgang eine Schublade auf. "Well, I **give in**. I guessed you'd decide to go to the island. You're just as **determined** as Bridget was. Once she'**d got a bee in her bonnet**, that was it ... But Laura, you don't know how popular that place is. It's always full of film stars and millionaires. It's an exclusive **resort** and people like us

---

My mind's made up. [maɪ ˌmaɪndz meɪd ˈʌp] Ich habe mich entschieden. **to give (gave, given) in** [ˌɡɪv / ˌɡeɪv / ˌɡɪvn ˈɪn] sich geschlagen geben **determined** [dɪˈtɜːmɪnd] entschlossen **to get (got, got) a bee in one's bonnet** [ɡet / ɡɒt / ɡɒt ə ˈbiː ɪn wʌnz ˈbɒnɪt] einen Floh im Ohr haben **resort** [rɪˈzɔːt] Urlaubsort

hardly **stand a chance** of getting a room there. However ..."
Milena war plötzlich aufgesprungen und sah Wolfgang mit großen Augen an. "Wolfie, you are good at **keeping secrets.** Is the spa where we're going next week for you to lose some weight the same spa that Laura's mother used to own?"
Ihr Mann verzog sein Gesicht zu einem schiefen Lausbubengrinsen. "Yes, it is, my darling. In September and October they're always closed for a while to **fix things up.** There are no paying guests – just friends of the family. And since I've known them so long, I am one of those friends. My wonderful assistant Michael **will take care of** the shop while we're away. And ... I booked an extra plane ticket because I was pretty sure that Laura would **insist on** coming along – once she'd looked in the box." Er zog drei Tickets aus der Schublade und wedelte mit ihnen in der Luft herum. "All three of us are going there!"
Entgeistert starrte Laura ihn an. "You actually know the people who **run** the spa?"
Wolfgang nickte. "I know them fairly well. Sylvie and Clive are both very nice. They were **devastated** when Bridget disappeared ... Oh, I've just remembered. I've got some photos of the island somewhere. You'll see how beautiful it is over there. Just wait until you see the **puffins!**"

---

to stand (stood, stood) a chance [ˌstænd / stʊd / stʊd ə ˈtʃɑːns] eine Chance haben **to keep (kept, kept) a secret** [ˌkiːp / ˌkept / ˌkept ə ˈsiːkrət] ein Geheimnis hüten **to fix things up** [ˌfɪks θɪŋz ˈʌp] Sachen in Ordnung bringen **to take (took, taken) care of sth.** [teɪk / tʊk / teɪkn ˈkeər əv] auf etw. aufpassen **to insist on sth.** [ɪnˈsɪst ɒn] auf etw. bestehen **to run (ran, run) sth.** [rʌn / ræn / rʌn] *hier*: etw. betreiben **devastated** [ˈdevəsteɪtɪd] am Boden zerstört **puffin** [ˈpʌfɪn] Papageientaucher

Und dann schauten sie sich Fotos an, bis Milena, trunken vom Champagner, ihren Kopf an Wolfgangs Schulter lehnte und leise zu schnarchen begann.

Übung 7: Was bedeuten die folgenden Redewendungen?

1. ☐ I've got a bee in my bonnet.
2. ☐ My mind's made up.
3. ☐ I'll leave no stone unturned.
4. ☐ My ears are burning.
5. ☐ To cut a long story short.
6. ☐ I sent him packing.
7. ☐ I took the plunge.
8. ☐ I can see it in my mind's eye.

a. ☐ I'll keep things brief.
b. ☐ I threw him out.
c. ☐ I'll do everything I can.
d. ☐ I did something that I was afraid of doing.
e. ☐ I'm determined.
f. ☐ I've made a decision.
g. ☐ Someone is talking about me.
h. ☐ I can imagine it.

Three

"Wow! We finally made it. I thought we **would** be **stuck** in that car for ever!", stöhnte Milena. "Just smell that sea **breeze**, Laura, and look at those waves!"
Laura stieg aus dem Mietwagen, in dem sie fünf Stunden lang gesessen hatten. Vom Flughafen in London Heathrow

---

to be (was, been) stuck [biː / wɒz / biːn ˈstʌk] festsitzen **breeze** [briːz] Brise waren sie hierher gefahren, zum Hafen von Penzance in Cornwall. Jetzt stand Laura still da und sog den Duft des Meeres ein. Sie hatte das eigenartige Gefühl, endlich nach Hause zu kommen.

Sie gingen an Bord eines schneeweißen Schiffes namens *The Scillonian*. Es lag bereits im Hafen und schien nur noch auf sie zu warten.

Laura schaute auf ihre Uhr. "It's two o'clock now. When do you think we'll arrive on Rose Island?"

"It'll take just over two and a half hours to get to St Mary's, the big island, and from there we'll take a smaller ferry over to Rose Island. I'm not sure whether we'll have to wait for the **tide**, but that trip will only take about half an hour. We should definitely get there by six p.m. at the latest."

Milena beugte sich über die Reling des Schiffs. "It's such a beautiful day. Why don't we go up to the top deck and see if we can grab a cappuccino and something to eat."

"That's a good idea. **I'm starving!** The sea air must be giving me an appetite."

Sie setzten sich auf das obere Deck, mit Blick auf das Festland und Wolfgang lächelte seinen beiden Begleiterinnen zu. "It's a real paradise for anyone who loves nature. I come here every year to go bird-watching. The climate on the islands is very mild because of the **Gulf Stream**. A lot of birds from America land on the islands for a rest before **migrating** further. You can't see these birds anywhere else in Europe!" Er hielt inne und ließ seinen Blick schweifen. "Just look at the coastline. See all those pretty seaside

---

tide [taɪd] Gezeiten **I'm starving!** [aɪm 'stɑːvɪŋ] Ich komme um vor Hunger! **Gulf Stream** ['gʌlf striːm] Golfstrom **to migrate** [maɪ'greɪt] fortziehen coves? The **Cornish** coast **used to be** full of smugglers. Rudyard Kipling, the guy who wrote *The Jungle Book*, was born near here. He wrote a song about smugglers with a **chorus** that goes like this:

Five and twenty ***ponies*** *trotting through the dark –*
Brandy *for the* ***Parson, baccy*** *for the Clerk,*
Laces *for a lady, letters for a* ***spy****,*
And watch the wall, my darling, while the ***gentlemen*** *go by!*"

Laura und Milena applaudierten begeistert.

Es war eine verrückte Vorstellung, dass die Vorfahren der Bewohner dieses wunderschönen Küstenstreifens Schmuggler gewesen waren. "So I guess I'**m descended from** a long line of smugglers!", staunte Laura.

Liebevoll, aber bestimmt schob Milena Wolfgang von der Bank. "I'm starving, and I'm sure Laura is too. Why don't you go and find some Cornish specialities for us? And don't forget the coffee, please."

Wolfgang nickte und kletterte kurz darauf die Treppen hinunter.

Übung 8: Wie viel wissen Sie über Cornwall?
Unterstreichen Sie die richtige Alternative.

1. Are the birds found on Cornish islands called **a.** puffins or **b.** parrots?
2. Does it take about **a.** five hours or **b.** ten hours to get from London to Cornwall?

Cornish ['kɔːnɪʃ] kornisch **used to be** ['juːst tə biː] war früher **chorus** ['kɔːrəs] Refrain **pony** ['pəʊnɪ] Pony **parson** ['pɑːsn] Pfarrer **baccy (tobacco)** ['bækɪ / tə'bækəʊ] Tabak **lace** [leɪs] Spitze **spy** [spaɪ] Spion **gentleman** ['dʒentlmən] Ehrenmann **to be (was, been) descended from sb.** [biː / wɒz / biːn dɪ'sendɪd frəm] von jmdm. abstammen

3. Does Cornwall have **a.** no coast or **b.** a coast?
4. Is Cornwall a paradise for **a.** cooks or **b.** bird-watchers?
5. Did Rudyard Kipling write **a.** *The Jogging Book* or **b.** *The Jungle Book?*

Das Schiff legte ab, und langsam entfernten sie sich vom Festland.
“See those white horses?”, schwärmte Milena. “That’s what we call it when we can see lots of waves with white **foam** on top. See! Don’t they just look like a **herd** of horses **rushing** along through the water, their **manes** dancing in the breeze?”
“I like that expression.” Wellen wie weiße Pferde. Nachdenklich fuhr sie mit ihrem Zeigefinger die kühle Reling entlang. “The *Scillonian*! Wasn’t that the name of the boat that my mother was last seen on?”
“Yes, as far as I remember, it had the same name. But that doesn’t mean it was exactly the same boat. – Laura, I’ve done some **research** for our mission.”
Sie hatte *our mission* gesagt. Verstohlen blickte Laura zu Milena, die verschiedene Prospekte aus ihrer Tasche hervorzauberte. Es fühlte sich gut an, nicht allein zu sein. In den letzten Tagen vor dem Abflug war es ihr erschienen, als habe sie plötzlich eine Familie gefunden.
“So, *carina*! **Here goes!**” Milena blätterte eines der Hefte durch, bis sie fand, was sie gesucht hatte, und las daraus vor.

---

foam [fəʊm] Schaum **herd** [hɜːd] Herde **to rush** [rʌʃ] stürmen
mane [meɪn] Mähne **research** [rɪˈsɜːtʃ] Nachforschungen
Here goes! [hɪə ˈgəʊz] Los geht’s!

"The Scilly Isles is a group of over 140 little **rocky** isles about 25 miles **southwest** of Land's End. Most of the islets are **deserted**, but some of the bigger ones are **inhabited**. The largest island is St Mary's, but it is only two and a half miles long from end to end. **Motor vehicles** are forbidden on all of the Scilly Isles."

"No cars?" Laura war begeistert. Das war Natur pur.
Milena nickte. "But listen to this. Doesn't this sound **weird**?"

The Scilly Isles have the largest concentration of neolithic **burial chambers** and stones in Europe."

Laura fröstelte. "That reminds me of my dream!", flüsterte sie. "In my dream I run past a **heap** of stones **leaning** against each other like a house of cards."
Milena blätterte in dem Heft, dann legte sie es aufgeschlagen vor Laura. "Like this?"

Laura blickte auf ein Bild, unter dem stand:

Neolithic burial chamber on the island of St Mary's.

Es verschlug ihr die Sprache. Die Steine auf dem Foto glichen fast haargenau denen in ihrem Traum. Mit einem Mal fühlte sie sich bedroht.

---

rocky ['rɒkɪ] felsig **southwest** [ˌsaʊθ'west] südwestlich **deserted** [dɪ'zɜːtɪd] unbewohnt **inhabited** [ɪn'hæbɪtɪd] bewohnt **motor vehicle** ['məʊtə ˌviːɪkl] Motorfahrzeug **weird** [wɪəd] seltsam **Neolithic** [ˌniːə'lɪθɪk] neolithisch **burial chamber** ['berɪəl ˌtʃeɪmbə] Grabkammer **heap** [hiːp] Haufen **to lean (leant, leant)** [liːn / lent / lent] (sich an)lehnen

Schritte aus Richtung der Treppe rissen sie aus ihren Gedanken. Wider Erwarten war es nicht Wolfgang mit einem Tablett voller Leckereien, sondern ein Mann mittleren Alters mit eingefetteter Langhaarfrisur, beigem Lederanzug und Cowboystiefeln. Er beachtete die beiden Frauen nicht, sondern stolzierte telefonierend an ihnen vorbei. Laura schnappte ein paar Fetzen des Gesprächs auf "Yes, I'm pretty sure they're selling the Ruby Rose Spa ..." Milena und Laura schauten sich überrascht an. "I don't know ... to a group of Americans. Soon, I think. They want to buy the whole island ..."

Laura hatte sich aufgerichtet und beobachtete den Mann. Er setzte sich an das andere Ende des Decks und war nunmehr außer Hörweite. Kurze Zeit später stand er auf und verschwand wieder unter Deck.

Laura und Milena starrten sich ungläubig an. "The Ruby Rose Spa! Rose Island!"

Aufgeregt durchforstete Milena ihren Prospektstapel.

"Here's a description."

Laura zog das Heft zu sich heran und las über die Einrichtung, die ihre Mutter vor vielen Jahren aufgebaut hatte und die möglicherweise jetzt an irgendwelche fremden Amerikaner verkauft werden sollte:

Übung 9: Setzen Sie das passende Wort ein.
*(opportunity, lose, luxury, according to, **including**, remote, mixture, weight)*

The Ruby Rose Spa located on the **1.** ______________

but beautiful Rose Island offers you the best **2.** ______________

---

including [ɪn'klu:dɪŋ] einschließlich

to relax and get away from it all. We have everything you need for a healthy, relaxing holiday – **3.** ______________ a large swimming pool as well as whirlpools in most rooms. We offer **4.** ______________ accommodation, lots of massage techniques, as well as world-class cuisine including, of course, our special Ruby Rose Soup, made for you **5.** ______________ a 300-year-old secret **6.** ______________ of powerful medicinal herbs. Many of our clients who come to the island with a **7.** ______________ problem **swear** that this soup helps them **8.** ______________ pounds ...

Irritiert sah Laura auf. "Ruby Rose Soup? Have you ever heard of it?"
"Apparently", sagte Milena, "lots of society people in New York swear by it."
Laura nickte gedankenverloren. Eine Suppe, mit der man abnehmen konnte, das klang nicht schlecht.

The spa and the island are now owned by Sylvie Stone, née Barée, the actress, famous for her role as Mademoiselle Lafleur in *Hearts Asunder*, the popular Seventies historical drama series. Mrs Sylvie Stone and her husband Dr Clive Stone run the spa together.

---

to swear (swore, sworn) [sweə / swɔː / swɔːn] schwören

"Here are some photos of the spa." Milena zog einige Fotos hervor und breitete sie auf dem Tisch aus. Laura betrachtete die Bilder des nah an den Klippen gelegenen Hotels. Eine unendlich lang erscheinende Treppe führte von einem kleinen Bootsanleger hinauf. Hinter dem einladenden, weißen Gebäude ragte ein Hügel auf.
"It seems to be located in a very **auspicious** place. It's facing the sea, but it isn't right on the edge of the cliff." Laura drehte eine Haarsträhne um ihren Zeigefinger. "There's plenty of room for the **phoenix** to fly. And there's a **protective turtle** behind the building."
Milena sah sie ratlos an. "What on earth are you talking about? Phoenix? Turtles? It sounds like **gibberish** to me! I don't understand a word!"
"Sorry! It's feng shui again!", lachte Laura. "All I mean is that the spa is in a great location. There's space for the phoenix to fly – that means that the spa has a clear view of the sea. The phoenix is a symbol of calm *chi* energy. And see that small hill, just behind the hotel? We call small hills like that turtles in feng shui. It's always good to have a 'turtle' – meaning **nurturing** *chi* energy – behind your house to protect it."
Milena nickte. "I see. It sounds as if the person who designed the hotel had a good intuitive **feel** for feng shui."
Laura folgte mit ihren Blicken einem Vogel. Ob die Planung des Hotels das Werk ihrer Mutter war? Hatte sie die Lust, Räume zu gestalten, von ihr geerbt? Konnte man so etwas überhaupt erben?

---

auspicious [ɔːˈspɪʃəs] vom Glück begünstigt **phoenix** [ˈfiːnɪks] Phoenix **protective** [prəˈtektɪv] schützend **turtle** [ˈtɜːtl] Schildkröte **gibberish** [ˈdʒɪbərɪʃ] Quatsch **nurturing** [ˈnɜːtʃərɪŋ] nährend **feel** [fiːl] Gefühl

Milena zupfte sie am Ärmel und deutete auf ein Bild in dem Prospekt. "Look! This must be Sylvie Stone and her husband Clive. She looks younger than I thought." Sie grinste. "But don't forget about the **miracles** of **cosmetic surgery**."
Jetzt betrachtete auch Laura das Gesicht der Frau auf dem Foto. "She has red hair and green eyes. She looks very glamorous. I wonder how she and my mother met?"
Milena strahlte. "Wolfie told me how they met. Apparently one day Sylvie was on a film shoot, and she lost her voice. None of the doctors could help her, and she had to give up **acting**. Later on, Bridget, who had already made something of a name for herself as a **herbalist**, made some special herbal tea for her. Apparently the tea tasted **foul**, but it worked. Sylvie got her voice back. But for some reason she never returned to acting. Of course, by that time she had met Dr Clive Stone and already fallen in love. Maybe that was the reason. In the meantime she and Bridget had become **bosom buddies**, and eventually Sylvie started to get really interested in health matters. Then she and Bridget **set up** this health resort on Rose Island."
Verblüfft schüttelte Laura ihren Kopf. "Is there no end to your knowledge, Milena?" Die beiden Frauen strahlten sich an, und in diesem Moment schnaufte Wolfgang die Treppe herauf und balancierte ein prall gefülltes Tablett mit Fleischpasteten und Kaffee darauf. "I'm sorry it took such a

---

cosmetic surgery [kɒzˌmetɪk ˈsɜːdʒərɪ] Schönheitschirurgie **acting** [ˈæktɪŋ] Schauspielerei **herbalist** [ˈhɜːbəlɪst] Kräuterheilkundige **foul** [faʊl] widerlich **bosom buddy** [ˈbʊzəm ˌbʌdɪ] Busenfreundin **to set (set, set) up sth.** [ˌset / ˌset / ˌset ˈʌp] etw. gründen long time. I met somebody I know at the bar. He's a friend of Clive and Sylvie's and he's on his way to Rose Island too. A **fellow** called Fred Lightfoot. He's a bit of an **oddball**. Fancies himself as Sioux **warrior**, I think. But you'll never guess what he just told me!"

"The spa's going to be sold!", antwortete Milena wie aus der Pistole geschossen.

Wolfgang starrte sie entgeistert an. "**Are** you **psychic** or something?"

"Just women's intuition, **honey**."

Laura war nicht nach Scherzen zumute. "Is he right, do you think?"

Ihr Onkel zuckte die Schultern. "Who knows? Let's buy him a drink later. Maybe we'll find out more. But for now just enjoy these delicious Cornish pasties. Cornish women used to make them for their husbands who worked down in the **tin mines**. Cornwell used to be famous for its tin mines."

"People don't **mine** tin here any more, but you can see the ruins of the **disused** mines all over the coast. People call them *Cornish castles*."

Milena nahm eine der Fleischpasteten und biss hinein. "**Yummy!** There are potatoes, carrots, peas and meat inside. **It's very filling.**"

---

fussy ['fʌsɪ] wählerisch **fellow** ['feləʊ] Kerl **oddball** ['ɒdbɔːl] komischer Kauz **warrior** ['wɒrɪə] Krieger **to be (was, been) psychic** [biː / wɒz / biːn 'saɪkɪk] hellsehen können **honey** ['hʌnɪ] *hier:* Süßer **tin mine** ['tɪn maɪn] Zinnbergwerk **to mine** [maɪn] abbauen **disused** [ˌdɪs'juːzd] stillgelegt **Yummy!** ['jʌmɪ] Lecker! **It's very filling.** [ɪts 'verɪ 'fɪlɪŋ] Es macht richtig satt.

Übung 10: Bringen Sie die Wörter in die richtige Reihenfolge.

1. actress spa owned the Sylvie now is by former Stone

____

2. attractive she an hair eyes red is woman and green with

____

3. lost acted never and her again voice she

____

4. famous used Cornwall for to mines tin be its

____

5. bit oddball Fred is of an Lightfoot a

____

6. vegetables filled meat pasties Cornish are with and

____

Plötzlich kam Laura ein ganz anderer Gedanke. "**Hold on!** What name shall I use when I introduce myself to people on the island? Laura Krüger or Rhiannon Krüger-Pencoe? Shall I introduce myself as Bridget's daughter?"
Milena und Wolfgang starrten sie an. Dann wischte sich Milena mit einer Serviette den Mund ab. "What a good question! If you introduce yourself as Bridget's daughter, and something **fishy** really did happen to Bridget . . . "

Hold on! [ˌhəʊld ˈɒn] Warte mal! **fishy** [ˈfɪʃɪ] *hier:* faul

Milena sprach den Gedanken nicht aus, aber alle drei wussten, was sie dachte. Falls einer der Anwesenden mit Bridgets Verschwinden zu tun hatte, was würde er oder sie tun, wenn ihre Tochter aus heiterem Himmel auftauchte? "Do you think Sylvie will recognize the name Laura Krüger?"
Wolfgang schüttelte den Kopf. "There isn't much chance of that. Martin and Bridget always called you Rhiannon. And Bridget didn't change her name to Krüger. But you look a lot like your mother. She might see a **resemblance**, who knows? I don't know what's best – keeping your identity a secret or telling everyone who you are."
Laura kaute auf ihren Lippen. "I'll just **play it by ear,** then." Sie schwieg einen Augenblick. "What happened to all the money my dad got when he sold the spa to Sylvie? He can't have spent it all on rum!"
Wolfgang schluckte sein letztes Stück Pasty hinunter. "After Martin sold everything off, he **fell in with a bad crowd** and started to **gamble. His debts mounted**. He was so **tormented** with **grief** when Bridget disappeared he just couldn't help himself. I tried to talk to him several months before he died. That's when he gave me the box. If only I **could have got through to** him somehow – but by that time he was **in a really bad way.**"

---

resemblance [rɪ'zembləns] Ähnlichkeit **to play it by ear** [ˌpleɪ ɪt baɪ 'ɪə] von Fall zu Fall entscheiden **to fall (fell, fallen) in with a bad crowd** [ˌfɔːl / ˌfel / ˌfɔːlən 'ɪn wɪð ə ˌbæd 'kraʊd] in schlechte Gesellschaft geraten **to gamble** ['gæmbl] (um Geld) spielen **His debts mounted.** [hɪz dets 'maʊntɪd] Sein Schuldenberg wuchs. **tormented** [tɔː'mentɪd] gequält **grief** [griːf] Gram **to get (got, got) through to sb.** [ˌget / ˌgɒt / ˌgɒt 'θruː tə] jmdn. erreichen **in a really bad way** [ɪn ə 'rɪəlɪ bæd ˌweɪ] in einer schlimmen Verfassung

Milena schüttelte traurig ihren Kopf. “What a **disaster**!”
“I wish he’d spent more time with me”, murmelte Laura.

Als sie kurz darauf in der Damentoilette ihr Gesicht im Spiegel inspizierte, zog sie ein kleines Parfümfläschchen aus ihrer Tasche hervor und betupfte sich damit. Das Fläschchen hatte sie erst zu Hause in der Schatulle ihres Vaters entdeckt. Es war versteckt gewesen, ganz unten, verhüllt in einem seidenen Tuch. Wohlig eingebettet in diesen Duft ging Laura kurz darauf zur Bar und setzte sich neben Wolfgang, der sich plötzlich irritiert umdrehte und jemanden zu suchen schien. Er schnupperte in die Luft und starrte schließlich Laura an. “That **scent** you’re wearing”, sagte er leise. “I recognize it.”
“I found it in the box.”
Wolfgang schluckte hart, und zum ersten Mal seit ihrer Begegnung sah Linda, dass Milena ihren Mann kritisch musterte.
“I’d know that scent anywhere. Bridget used to experiment with all kinds of natural **remedies** and cosmetics. She was trying to develop a new kind of perfume using **ancient** texts. She had an old book of herbal recipes that she **had inherited**, which she often used as an inspiration. She created that perfume herself. She was wearing it the last time I saw her.”
Milenas Augen verdunkelten sich. “When exactly did you last see her, Wolfie?”
Bildete Laura es sich nur ein, oder schwang Eifersucht in Milenas Stimme mit?
Zögernd antwortete Wolfgang. “I was on the island, you

---

disaster [dɪ'zɑːstə] Unglück **scent** [sent] Duft **remedy** ['remədɪ] Heilmittel **ancient** ['eɪnʃənt] uralt **to inherit** [ɪn'herɪt] erben know, that December when she vanished. Bridget was quite busy, as the spa was really booming. I left for Hamburg a couple of days before she did." Wolfgang hielt einen Moment inne. Mit belegter Stimme fügte er dann hinzu: "She was wearing that perfume when we said goodbye . . ."

"Just how well did you know her, Wolfgang?" Doch noch ehe Wolfgang antworten konnte, wandte Milena sich abrupt von ihrem Mann ab und ihr zu. "Oh, I'm sorry, Laura – I didn't mean . . . For a moment there, I'd forgotten she was your mother."

Laura schüttelte lächelnd den Kopf und bemühte sich, gleichgültig zu wirken. Aber in ihr kreiste alles Denken und Fühlen um dieselbe Frage: Was war zwischen Wolfgang und ihrer Mutter passiert?

Wolfgang blickte von ihr zu Milena. "Don't worry, we were just very good friends. She and Martin were happy together. I would never ever have . . ."

Ein kräftiger Ruck ging durch den Schiffsrumpf, und er verstummte. Die *Scillonian* hatte am Kai angelegt, sie waren auf St Mary's Island gelandet.

Übung 11: Welche Wörter gehören zusammen?

1. soft	☐	**a.** remedy
2. Cornish	☐	**b.** location
3. herbal	☐	**c.** pasty
4. tin	☐	**d.** shoot
5. women's	☐	**e.** buddy
6. film	☐	**f.** mine
7. cosmetic	☐	**g.** intuition
8. bosom	☐	**h.** goods
9. remote	☐	**i.** surgery
10. smuggled	☐	**j.** toy

Four

Sie gingen in einem kleinen Hafen von Bord. Bunte Boote schaukelten auf dem unruhigen Wasser. Laura sah sich begeistert um. "This place is amazing", schwärmte sie. Wolfgang begutachtete unterdessen den kleinen Fahrplan. Milena stand neben dem Gepäck und starrte, in Gedanken versunken, auf die Wellen.

Wolfgang blickte besorgt zu Milena und dann zum Himmel. "I think the clouds from the Atlantic **are moving in.** The helicopter service to Rose Island doesn't run when the weather's stormy."

Ihre Blicke verfingen sich ineinander, dann erschien ein Lächeln auf Milenas Gesicht.

"What, no helicopter! Do you mean that all these poor rich people **have to put up with** two boat **rides**!" Milena schien wieder zu ihrer guten Laune zurückzufinden, und Laura sah erleichtert, wie Wolfgang seine Frau anlächelte. Dann lief Milena zu ihm, und er nahm sie in seine Arme.

"Come on", hörte sie Milena leise zu ihm sagen, "It's not your fault Bridget disappeared. You probably **couldn't have prevented** it. But now we can try to help Laura find out the truth!"

"You're right, darling."

Milena löste sich von ihm und nahm ihre Umgebung wieder wahr. "It's like paradise!"

Dann stupste sie Laura an und zeigte auf eine kleine Barkasse. "Do you see what I see? That boat over there is called *The Turtle*!"

---

to move in [ˌmuːv ˈɪn] anrücken **to put (put, put) up with sth.** [ˌpʊt / ˌpʊt / ˌpʊt ˈʌp wɪð] sich mit etw. abfinden **ride** [raɪd] Fahrt **to prevent** [prɪˈvent] verhindern

"That's our boat", rief Wolfgang. "It's **ahead** of schedule!" Schon von Weitem fiel Laura eine gut aussehende, rothaarige Frau an Bord der Barkasse auf.
"That's Sylvie Stone", sagte Wolfgang überrascht und lief vor. Laura hätte Sylvie am liebsten umgehend zu den Verkaufsplänen befragt, doch Milena hielt sie zurück und flüsterte: "Hold on! Let me **handle** it. I am the journalist here, after all. I'm good at **getting to the bottom of** things."
Vielleicht hatte sie recht, auch wenn es Laura nicht leicht fiel, sich zu gedulden. Wolfgang begrüßte jetzt Sylvie Stone, die ihrem Bild in dem Prospekt tatsächlich sehr ähnlich sah. "It's good to see you again. I'm **honoured** that you've come to St Mary's to welcome us in person."
Sylvie Stone lächelte charmant und umarmte ihn. "It's always a pleasure to welcome you, Wolfgang. You are one of our oldest guests, after all."
Laura glaubte eine Spur französischen Akzents in ihrer Sprache herauszuhören. Ob Sylvie Stone Französin war?
In diesem Moment drehte Sylvie sich um und schaute sie an. Sie sah recht jung aus, und ihre Augen glitzerten mit ihrem Smaragdschmuck um die Wette. "And you must be Milena, Wolfgang's new Eve from the Big Apple!"
Wolfgang lachte und zog Milena zu sich. "No, I'm afraid you're wrong for once, Sylvie. This is Milena."
Milena lächelte höflich und reichte Sylvie die Hand.
"I **adore** the States", plauderte diese unbeirrt weiter. "Everything is so much more liberal over there, don't you think?"

---

ahead [ə'hed] vor **to handle sth.** ['hændl] umgehen mit etw.
to get (got, got) to the bottom of sth. [ˌget / gɒt / gɒt tə ðə 'bɒtəm əv] einer Sache auf den Grund gehen **honoured** ['ɒnəd] geehrt
to adore [ə'dɔː] (innig) lieben

"Like the **gun laws**!" Milenas lakonischer Humor und ihre Schlagfertigkeit schienen sie wirklich in keiner Situation zu verlassen.

Übung 12: Bilden Sie die Vergleichsform (Komparativ).

1. The gun laws are *(liberal)* more liberal ______ in America than in Europe.

2. Rose Island is *(far)* ______ away from the mainland than St Mary's.

3. Feng shui is *(well-known)* ______ in Hong Kong than in Europe.

4. Rhiannon is a *(interesting)* ______ name than Laura.

5. Laura is *(knowledgeable)* ______ about feng shui than Milena.

6. Milena is *(sociable)* ______ than Laura.

7. Milena is *(fussy)* ______ about coffee than Wolfgang.

8. Tomorrow the weather will be *(bad)* ______ than today.

9. It's *(good)* ______ to be safe than sorry.

---

gun law [ˈgʌn lɔː] Waffengesetz

Dann zog Wolfgang Laura zu sich heran. “And this is the friend I was telling you about. Thanks for making an extra room **available at** such **short notice.**”

Laura reichte ihr die Hand. “My name is . . . Laura Krüger. Pleased to meet you, Mrs Stone.”

Sylvie sah sie aufmerksam an, und Laura hatte den Eindruck, als hielte sie ihre Hand etwas länger als üblich in der ihren. “Welcome, Laura. I hope you’ll enjoy our little island. You look so **familiar.** Are you on T.V. or in the movies?”

Sie schüttelte den Kopf und entzog Sylvie ihre Hand. “No, I’m nobody special, Mrs Stone!”

“Don’t be so modest, Laura”, kam Milena ihr zu Hilfe. “You’re not only a wonderful interior designer but also one of the best feng shui experts in Germany.”

Mit ihrer Bemerkung schien sie ins Schwarze getroffen zu haben, denn Sylvie war gleich Feuer und Flamme. “Wow! Feng shui! That sounds interesting!” Dann fügte sie verschwörerisch hinzu: “And please do call me Sylvie! Calling me Mrs Stone makes me sound like a fossil! By the way”, Sylvie hielt inne und wandte sich einem Mann zu, der mit seinem Gepäck auf die *Turtle* zueilte. Laura und Milena blickten einander erschrocken an. Es war der Mann, den sie auf dem Schiff ungewollt belauscht hatten. Sylvie hatte ihre Irritation nicht bemerkt und fuhr mit Blick auf den Mann in Leder fort. “Have you met Mr Fred Lightfoot yet? He was on the *Scillonian*, too.”

Fred Lightfoot hielt kurz inne und schüttelte den Anwe-

---

available [ə'veɪləbl] verfügbar **at short notice** [ət ʃɔːt 'nəʊtɪs] kurzfristig **familiar** [fə'mɪlɪə] bekannt senden die Hand, ohne in ihre Augen zu sehen. Dann setzte er seinen Weg fort.

Sylvie erklärte mit verhaltener Stimme: "Fred Lightfoot is very spiritually oriented. **He's into meditation in a big way.**"

Ein kleiner, drahtiger Mann um die fünfzig drängte sich nun ungefragt zwischen sie und unterbrach barsch das Gespräch. "Are we ready to **weigh anchor**, Ma'am? I'd like to catch the tide, if you don't mind."

Sylvie schien die Unfreundlichkeit des Mannes nicht persönlich zu nehmen. "Oh, I'm sorry, Ted. Excuse me for a moment, everybody, please. I'd just like to make sure all the luggage **has been properly stowed away.**"

Als Sylvie sich nun umwandte und dem Kapitän des Schiffes folgte, sah Laura, wie dieser ihr einen kleinen Leinenbeutel zusteckte, den sie schnell in ihrer Tasche verschwinden ließ.

Unterdessen quälte sich Wolfgang durch die schmale Öffnung in die Passagierkabine hinab. Milena wisperte hinter vorgehaltener Hand Laura zu: "Don't you think that Ted looks just like one of those old Cornish smugglers Wolfgang was telling us about?"

Aber Laura hatte Fred Lightfoot entdeckt, der sich im Schneidersitz in eine Ecke gesetzt hatte und ganz abwesend schien. Sylvie, die ihre Unterredung mit dem Kapitän beendet hatte, gesellte sich zu ihnen und flüsterte: "Fred can sit like this for ages. Then he'll stop and suddenly ask for coffee. Why don't we sit down and have something hot to drink. Coffee? Tea? Hot chocolate?"

He's into meditation in a big way. [hɪːz ɪntə ˌmedɪˈteɪʃn ɪn ə ˈbɪg ˌweɪ] 'Er steht voll auf Meditation.' **to weigh anchor** [weɪ ˈæŋkə] den Anker lichten **properly** [ˈprɒpəlɪ] ordnungsgemäß **to stow sth. away** [ˌstəʊ əˈweɪ] etw. verstauen

Milena und Laura nickten begeistert. Endlich gab es Kaffee! Sylvie zog eine große Thermosflasche und einige Plastikbecher aus einem Korb, und sie ließen sich in einiger Entfernung von Fred Lightfoot auf eine Bank nieder. "I'm sorry it's not the Ritz", meinte Sylvie entschuldigend, "but I promise things will be a bit more luxurious on the island. The trip will take about half an hour. When Fred's finished . . . meditating, he'll join us."

Das Boot legte ab. Wolfgang gesellte sich wieder zu ihnen, und sie machten es sich gemütlich. Milena geriet bereits nach dem ersten Schluck Kaffee ins Schwärmen: "Yes, Arabica beans! Freshly **ground**! Delicious!"

Unauffällig beobachtete Laura Sylvie. Sie war eine Freundin ihrer Mutter gewesen, vielleicht sogar ihre beste Freundin. Sie hatte ein Recht darauf zu wissen, wer Laura war.

Doch noch ehe sie etwas sagen konnte, ergriff Milena das Wort: "What about this Ruby Rose Soup? Does it really work?"

Sylvie nickte verschmitzt. "Our customers think so! Everyone seems *très* happy." Das französische Wort passte zu ihr und wirkte sympathisch.

"What goes into the soup then?" Milena blieb hartnäckig.

"Now, now; that would be telling. But okay, if you really want to know, the soup **contains** water, salt and pepper and ... a few other **ingredients**!"

Milena verzog das Gesicht, aber Sylvie ging charmant darüber hinweg: "Actually, the exact recipe *is* a secret. I always like to say that it is the best-kept secret in the world – even more secret than the recipe for Coca-Cola. I make the

---

ground [graʊnd] gemahlen **to contain** [kən'teɪn] enthalten
ingredients [ɪn'griːdɪənts] Zutaten

soup personally every day. Apart from my husband Clive I am the only one who knows exactly what goes into it."

Milena zog eine ihrer unzähligen Broschüren hervor. "In the picture it looks extremely red. Is it made with tomatoes or **seaweed** or red **cabbage** or something?"

Ungläubig schüttelte Sylvie den Kopf. "Cabbage? Seaweed? Oh, you don't give up, do you!"

"Milena is a reporter. She can't help asking lots of questions." Entschuldigend lächelte Laura Sylvie an.

Sylvie schien begeistert. "That's very interesting! Now I understand why you're so **curious**, Milena." Ihr Blick wanderte zu Laura zurück. "What about you, Laura? Do you have any questions?"

Laura zögerte. "I've read that this soup was originally made by somebody else – a woman by the name of Bridget Pencoe."

Sylvie erstarrte, ihre Pupillen weiteten sich, und sie schwieg einige Augenblicke, ehe die Worte wie ein Wasserfall aus ihr herausströmten.

Übung 13: Setzen Sie die richtige Alternative ein.

"Bridget. Oh, she was such a **1.** ______________ *(bad/dear)* friend. We . . . we were like sisters. We didn't look like sisters, of course." Sie lächelte, und ihr Blick verlor sich in den unruhigen Wellen des Meeres, während ihre Hände beim Erzählen Seemöwen gleich durch die Luft tanzten.

---

seaweed ['si:wi:d] Seetang **cabbage** ['kæbɪdʒ] Kohl **curious** ['kjʊərɪəs] neugierig

"I have red **2.** ____________ *(hairs/hair)*, and she had **3.** ____________ *(blond/blonde)* hair. But we were about the same **height**. We **4.** ____________ *(got/became)* very close friends. She was a herbalist, and she had this **5.** ____________ *(strange/expensive)* book that she inherited from her mother and grandmother. There were lots of **6.** ____________ *(receipts/recipes)* in there for all sorts of things. When I was still playing the role of Mademoiselle Lafleur, I lost my voice. I was desperate! Nobody **7.** ____________ *(rents/hires)* an actress who's lost her voice! The doctors were very surprised. But Bridget helped. She found a **8.** ____________ *(verbal/herbal)* recipe in her book and **9.** ____________ *(spared/saved)* my voice for me. I really loved her ... And you're right, of course. She was the one who developed the Ruby Rose **10.** ____________ *(Soap/Soup)*."

Die Vogelhände fielen herab und rollten sich traurig in Sylvies Schoß zusammen. "Without her I would be nothing. There would be no Ruby Rose Spa ... We made such great

---

height [haɪt] Größe

plans. We wanted to try out all kinds of different recipes. Face creams, perfumes, lots of things. But one day she just . . ." Sylvie schluckte, und Laura hing an ihren Lippen, obschon sie wusste, was nun kommen würde. "She just vanished **without a trace**! It was . . . tragic. She left a little girl and a husband behind, you know. Nobody has any idea what happened to her – even to this day. I . . . still . . . miss her."
Kurz fragte Laura sich, warum Sylvie sich nie nach ihr, Laura, erkundigt hatte. Oder hatte es vielleicht Versuche gegeben, und ihre Großmutter hatte sie unterbunden?
"She disappeared, you say? But who was the last person to see her?", platzte es aus Laura heraus. Objektiv betrachtet, war die Frage viel zu direkt gestellt, doch Sylvie schien zu sehr mit ihren eigenen Gedanken beschäftigt, um es zu bemerken. "My husband, Clive. He took her by boat from Rose Island to St Mary's. Clive left her on St Mary's, and some people saw her board the *Scillonian* for Penzance. She was on her way to join her daughter and husband in Germany. But then . . . she simply vanished into thin air. Nobody ever saw her again. She left no note or letter . . . nothing." Die Worte brachen aus ihr heraus, als sei ein Staudamm in ihrem Inneren geöffnet worden. "I'm sorry, Laura. You must be wondering what's wrong with me. I . . ."
Laura schüttelte den Kopf. "It's okay. Really. I . . . There's something I want to tell you . . . I . . ."
Aber in diesem Augenblick tauchte Fred Lightfoot neben Sylvie auf, und Laura verstummte. Noch ganz abwesend ließ er sich neben Sylvie auf die Bank gleiten und nippte träumend an seinem Kaffee. Laura stand auf. "I'm tired of sitting around. I'll have a walk around the boat."

---

without a trace [wɪðˌaʊt ə ˈtreɪs] spurlos

Zu ihrer Überraschung schloss sich Sylvie ihr dankbar an. “That’s a brilliant idea. Let’s see if we can make out Rose Island on the horizon yet!”
Sie waren erst wenige Schritte gegangen, als das Boot plötzlich durch einen hohen Wellengang stark zu schaukeln begann. Sylvie schwankte und wäre beinahe hingefallen, wenn Laura sie nicht gestützt hätte. “Sorry”, entschuldigte sie sich und wollte sich schon wieder aufrichten, als sie plötzlich innehielt und Laura verwundert anstarrte. “That scent – I’d know that scent anywhere!” Mit fliegendem Blick sah sie sich um und klammerte sich an die Reling.
Laura errötete. Sie roch offensichtlich immer noch nach dem Parfum ihrer Mutter.
Sylvie keuchte. “Bridget? . . . No, it can’t be! Who are you? You’ve got Bridget’s eyes . . . Is that you . . . Rhiannon?” Sylvies Stimme zitterte.
Laura nickte. “That’s what I was trying to tell you before, Sylvie. It’s me, Rhiannon. Rhiannon Laura Pencoe-Krüger. Bridget’s daughter. I’ve come here to find out what happened to my mother.”
Wolfgang und Milena waren ihnen gefolgt. Sie kamen gerade noch rechtzeitig, um die in Ohnmacht fallende Sylvie aufzufangen. Milena schaute Laura fragend an. “You told her, didn’t you?”

Five

Wolfgang, Milena und Laura hatten Sylvie auf eine Bank gelegt. Langsam kam sie wieder zu sich, blinzelte und schaute direkt in Lauras Gesicht. Dann huschte ein Lächeln über ihre noch bleichen Züge. “I just can’t believe it. Rhiannon! After all these years!” Langsam und vorsichtig rich-

tete sie sich auf. "I tried to get in touch with you – but nobody ever answered our letters or calls. I never thought I'd see Bridget's little daughter again."
Noch ehe Laura antworten konnte, schallte Teds raue Stimme über das Deck: "Rose Island **ahoy!**"
Die Silhouette einer Insel tauchte aus dem Blau des Meeres am Horizont auf und kam schnell näher. Laura spürte ein Kribbeln im ganzen Körper. Das war die Insel ihrer Mutter.
Sylvie richtete sich auf, und Wolfgang half ihr dabei. "Yes, we're here. Normally, it takes much longer to get here, but today the **current** is quite strong."
Milena nickte, warf Laura einen kurzen Blick zu und fragte dann: "I heard a **rumour** that you're going to sell the spa and the island. Is that true?"
Sylvie wirkte wie vom Donner gerührt. Für einen kurzen Augenblick befürchtete Laura, sie würde erneut in Ohnmacht fallen. Stattdessen aber sagte sie kraftlos: "It's complicated. Let's talk about it later."
Milena nickte, als sei ihr das Thema nicht wichtig.
Mit einem Blick auf Laura fügte Sylvie hinzu: "And we both have a lot to talk about, my dear ... if you want to, that is."
"I'd love to", lächelte Laura.
"Okay then." Sylvie stand langsam und vorsichtig auf und strich ihre Kleidung glatt. "I'll see you in a minute." Mit diesen Worten drehte sie sich um und ging in Richtung Kapitänskajüte. Laura sah ihr nach, bis ihre schlanke Gestalt im Inneren des Schiffes verschwunden war.

---

ahoy! [ə'hɔɪ] ahoi! **current** ['kʌrənt] Strömung **rumour** ['ruːmə] Gerücht

Übung 14: Beantworten Sie folgende Fragen zum Text.

1. How did Sylvie manage to recognize Laura?

____

2. Why did they arrive at the island so early?

____

3. Who are the only two people who know the recipe for the soup?

____

4. Who originally developed the recipe?

____

5. Who was the last person to see Bridget Pencoe?

____

6. Did Sylvie try to get in touch with Laura after Bridget disappeared?

____

Die *Turtle* näherte sich nun ziemlich schnell der Insel, und Laura betrachtete das Ufer mit klopfendem Herzen.
"See how high the cliff is!", rief Milena begeistert und zeigte auf das weiße Gebäude, das hoch oben auf den Klippen thronte.
Wolfgang hatte sein Fernglas ausgepackt. "Look at the **flocks** of birds flying **overhead**. I can't wait to get closer."

---

flock [flɒk] Schwarm **overhead** ['əʊvəhed] (dr)oben

Milena lehnte sich an Laura und wisperte ihr zu: "Well, I'm glad we made it. I'm starting to feel a little sick. I'm not much of a sailor, I'm afraid."
Laura lächelte ihr aufmunternd zu. "I just love it – I think I inherited my Dad's **sea legs**."
Wolfgang, der immer noch durch sein Fernglas starrte, zeigte auf den Anleger. "There's somebody waiting for us."
Wie aus dem Nichts war Sylvie erneut hinter ihnen. "It's Clive. I told him to meet us." Sie sah zum Ufer, dann murmelte sie enttäuscht: "Oh, it's just Peter Saunders. It's easy to **mistake** the two of them at a distance. They're about the same size and both of them have dark hair."
"Who's Peter Saunders?"
He's just started working for us as a fitness instructor. I go jogging with him every morning at seven. You're welcome to join us if you like."
Laura war begeistert. "I love jogging but I'm not really such an **early bird**. Maybe we can go jogging in the evening instead."
"That would be lovely." Sylvie nickte ihr zu und blieb etwas zu lange an Lauras Augen hängen. Dann schüttelte sie ergriffen den Kopf und lächelte sanft, bevor sie sich abwandte.
Als die *Turtle* anlegte, sprang Ted als erster ans Ufer und half Sylvie und den Gästen an Land. Peter Saunders, ein sehr attraktiver Mann mit auffallend warmen, braunen Augen und dunklem, vom Wind zerzaustem Schopf, hieß sie freundlich willkommen. Sein Händedruck war kräftig, aber angenehm, und sein Körper, so fand Laura, atembe-

---

sea legs ['siː legz] *hier:* Seefestigkeit **to mistake (mistook, mistaken)** [mɪs'teɪk / mɪs'tʊk / mɪs'teɪkən] verwechseln **early bird** ['ɜːlɪ bɜːd] Frühaufsteherin raubend. Während er sprach, konnte Laura kaum den Blick von ihm wenden. Kurz: Er war ein waschechter Märchenprinz. Das hatte ihr gerade noch gefehlt. Märchenprinzen in ihrem Leben waren stets ungesund gewesen. Unwillig schüttelte sie den Kopf und zwang sich, ihren Blick von ihm ab und Milena zuzuwenden.

"Not bad looking, eh?", flüsterte Sylvie, während Ted und Wolfgang mit Peters Hilfe begannen, das Gepäck auszuladen. "How about an early morning jog with him? **Tempting**, isn't it?"

Laura verdrehte die Augen. "No, thanks. He's a little too perfect for me."

Dann vernahmen sie einen tiefen Brummton. Er kam von Fred Lightfoot, der sich seinen Weg zwischen ihnen hindurchbahnte. "O Great **Spirit** of the island, I am your **humble servant**", murmelte er und schritt den Fußweg entlang in Richtung Treppe, ohne einen der Umstehenden auch nur eines Blickes zu würdigen.

"Did he just say what I think he said? That man is weird. Even by New York standards!", murmelte Milena.

"Fred believes that spirits live on this island", entschuldigte ihn Sylvie. "Sometimes he wanders off by himself for hours."

Dann wandte sie sich an Peter: "Where's Clive? He said he'd meet us here."

Peter zuckte mit den Schultern. "I guess he might be out jogging or something. You've arrived back really early. I just happened to be out on the cliff **path** and saw you arriving. Nobody was expecting you to get here this quickly." Er

---

tempting ['temptɪŋ] verlockend **spirit** ['spɪrɪt] Geist **humble** ['hʌmbl] ergeben **servant** ['sɜːvənt] Diener **path** [pɑːθ] Pfad

griff sich Lauras Koffer und eine Tasche, lächelte Laura an und folgte Fred Lightfoot.
Ted trieb derweil zur Eile an. "There's a storm **brewing**. It'll hit us tonight or tomorrow morning at the very latest. I hope you've got enough **supplies** because you might be **cut off** for a day or more. **I'll be off** as soon as we've **unloaded** everything.
Sylvie nickte, dann wandte sie sich ihren Gästen zu.
"Don't worry!" Sie schien die Anwensenden beruhigen zu wollen, obwohl die Ankündigung des Sturms niemanden zu beunruhigen schien. "Our head chef Jean-Paul is always very good about **stocking up**. We've got a giant **cold storage room** packed with food. Jean-Paul even stocks frozen pizza for emergencies. Better safe than sorry!"
Laura folgte Sylvies Blick, der wieder und wieder die Klippen nach ihrem Mann absuchte.
"Wolfgang, why don't we let Peter take the two ladies up while you and I **stretch** our legs and go and look for Clive. There are some rare birds **nesting** just over there."
Laura verspürte einen kleinen Stich, weil Sylvie nicht sie gefragt hatte, aber Wolfgang stimmte begeistert zu. "Great idea, Sylvie! I hope you don't mind, Milena? Laura?"
Mit einem Seitenblick auf Milena verneinte auch Laura, und Sylvie und Wolfgang ließen sie mit Peter Saunders allein, der gerade die Treppe heruntergesprintet kam und sich nun Milenas Koffern zuwandte. Als er den ersten anhob, ächzte er zum Spaß unter dem Gewicht.

---

to brew [bruː] *hier:* in der Luft liegen **supplies** [səˈplaɪz] Vorrat **cut off** [ˌkʌt ˈɒf] abgeschnitten **I'll be off** [ˌaɪl bɪ ˈɒf] Ich werde weggehen **to unload** [ʌnˈləʊd] ausladen **to stock up** [ˌstɒk ˈʌp] Vorräte anlegen **cold storage room** [kəʊld ˈstɔːrɪdʒ ruːm] Kühlraum **to stretch** [stretʃ] strecken **to nest** [nest] nisten

Dann strich er sich die Haare aus den Augen und ließ grinsend seine Muskeln spielen. “It’s good weight training **at any rate.**” Er hob die zwei großen Koffer an und überholte Milena. “This way, ladies.”
Während sie Peter Saunders folgten, bewunderte Laura selbstvergessen seinen durchtrainierten Rücken.
Milena bleckte die Zähne. “That guy is a sexbomb, isn’t he?”
“And”, knurrte Laura, “he knows it!”

Übung 15: Yin und Yang sind Gegensätze.
Suchen Sie die Gegensätze heraus.

1. thin	☐	**a.**	arrogant
2. fat	☐	**b.**	common
3. often	☐	**c.**	small
4. rare	☐	**d.**	thick
5. near	☐	**e.**	thin
6. early bird	☐	**f.**	remote
7. huge	☐	**g.**	rarely
8. modest	☐	**h.**	**night owl**

Six

Während Laura und Milena keuchten, als sie den Gipfel erreicht hatten, wirkte Peter ganz ruhig und entspannt.
“So, what are your first **impressions**?” Er hatte die Koffer abgestellt und wartete geduldig auf die beiden Frauen.
Laura drehte sich einmal langsam um sich selbst. Als sie zum Spa schaute, erschrak sie. Der Weg führte von den

---

at any rate [ət 'enɪ reɪt] jedenfalls **night owl** ['naɪt aʊl] Nachtmensch **impression** [ɪm'preʃn] Eindruck

Treppen aus schnurgerade auf den Eingang des Hauses zu.
"**What's the matter?**", wunderte sich Peter.
"Well, it's nothing really. Just that the path leading up to the front door is straight. Straight lines aren't good in feng shui, especially when they lead up to doors. The Chinese believe that bad energy called *sh'a* moves easily along straight lines. They always try to make their paths **curved instead of** straight. If I were advising Sylvie, I'd get her to change the shape of the path." Sie grinste, als sie in Peters völlig verständnisloses Gesicht schaute. "In feng shui any kind of straight line that **points to** a sensitive **spot** is called a 'killing **arrow**'. It doesn't kill you literally, of course".
Plötzlich wurde die Tür des Hauses aufgerissen, und eine ältere, elegant gekleidete Dame trat heraus. Laura zuckte zusammen. Die Frau stand sozusagen mitten in der Schusslinie. Sie schüttelte die Gedanken ab, schließlich hatte so ein 'killing arrow' – wenn überhaupt – erfahrungsgemäß nur so etwas wie Kopfschmerzen zur Folge. Peter hingegen musste sie jetzt für verrückt halten. Nun ja, es sollte ihr recht sein. Schließlich hatte sie sich ja vorgenommen, in ihrem Leben auf Märchenprinzen zu verzichten.
"Welcome", rief die Frau ihnen zu. "Welcome to the Ruby Rose Spa. You've arrived a little ahead of schedule. But do please come inside. My name is Alison Rutherford. I'm the hotel receptionist and clerk."

Sie betraten die Eingangshalle, wo die kleine, quirlige Mrs. Rutherford hinter ihren Empfangstresen lief und ein großes

---

What's the matter? [ˌwɒts ðə ˈmætə] Was ist los? **curved** [ˈkɜːvd] gebogen **instead of** [ɪnˈsted əv] (an)statt von **to point to sth.** [ˈpɔɪnt tə] auf etw. deuten **spot** [spɒt] Stelle **arrow** [ˈærəʊ] Pfeil

Buch aufschlug. Hinter ihr war eine Stellwand aufgebaut, vermutlich damit sie sich zurückziehen konnte. Daneben stand eine schmale antike Glasvitrine mit lauter Sternzeichen-Souvenirs. Mrs. Rutherford plapperte munter drauflos. “Are you Mrs Kaden? You work in New York, don’t you? I’ve never been to America but I would love to go there! Especially to New York, the ‘Big Apple’. Mrs Stone adores it.”
Während Milena und Mrs. Rutherford die Vor- und Nachteile von New York erörterten, sah Laura sich um. Sie befanden sich im Mittelpunkt einer lichten, kreisrunden Kuppelhalle, von der sternförmig Gänge in verschiedenen Farben abgingen. Die Eingangstür flankierten zwei schneeweiße Statuen, ein Mann und eine Frau, griechischen Götterstatuen gleich. Die Lobby wurde offensichtlich auch als Café benutzt; ein Dutzend Tischchen mit Stühlen waren dezent durch Palmen voneinander abgeschirmt. Laura spähte in einen der Gänge und konnte zwei Türschilder ausmachen: ‘Diane Bragg, Personal Assistant’ und ‘Sylvie and Dr Clive Stone’.
Mrs. Rutherford quasselte noch immer. “You must visit the gardens. They’re full of herbs and subtropical orchids.”
Milena hatte sich in das Buch eingetragen, drehte sich zu Laura und reichte ihr Augen rollend den Stift.
Mrs. Rutherford sah Laura aufmerksam an. “Have we met before? You look so familiar. Maybe you’re a movie star or something? Please sign here. You don’t have to fill in your **date of birth** if you don’t want to! Most women who come here don’t do it. But my hobby’s astrology, you know. My birthday is the first of April – **April Fools’ Day**. That makes

---

date of birth [ˌdeɪt əv ˈbɜːθ] Geburtsdatum **April Fool’s day** [ˈeɪprəl fuːlz deɪ] der erste April me **Aries**. Aries happens to be the first sign in the Zodiac", sagte sie stolz. "If you're interested in astrology, I can book you in for an astrological **consultation** with Diane Bragg. That's Mrs Stone's P.A. – Personal Assistant. She's also a professional astrologer . . ."

Übung 16: Astrology Quiz

Are the stars important for you?

Unterstreichen Sie Ihre Antwort.

1. Do you ever read your horoscope in the newspaper? *(Yes/No)*
2. Do you know what sign of the zodiac you are? *(Yes/No)*
3. Have you ever had your horoscope done? *(Yes/No)*
4. Have you ever visited somebody who knows a lot about astrology? *(Yes/No)*
5. Do you know if your partner's sign of the zodiac is a good one for you? *(Yes/No)*
6. Do you know what animal you are in Chinese astrology? *(Yes/No)*
7. Have you ever felt unhappy because your horoscope was bad? *(Yes/No)*
8. Do you own a book about astrology? *(Yes/No)*
9. Do you have a computer programme for horoscopes? *(Yes/No)*
10. Have you ever made an important decision because of your horoscope? *(Yes/No)*

Mrs. Rutherford zog aus einer der Schubladen ein kleines Büchlein mit unzähligen Namen und Geburtsdaten. "When-

---

Aries ['eərɪ:z] Widder **consultation** [ˌkɒnsl'teɪʃn] Beratung
astrology [ə'strɒlədʒɪ] Astrologie

ever I meet anyone, I try to make a note of their date of birth – especially the **celebrities**. Did you know that Madonna . . . ”

Laura hörte nur mit halbem Ohr zu, zögerte eine Weile, dann schrieb sie ‘R. Laura Krüger’ und notierte ihr Geburtsdatum. Anschließend fiel ihr Blick auf Peter, der wartend neben den Koffern stand und sie die ganze Zeit beobachtet hatte.

Er lächelte sie an. Laura schmolz dahin wie Eis in der Sonne. Sie wurde feuerrot und wandte sich abrupt ab. Ob Peter mit allen Frauen so flirtete? Mrs. Rutherford hatte ihr Interesse an Laura verloren und zeigte Milena gerade die Ketten mit den Sternzeichenanhängern in der Vitrine. Sie öffnete die Glastür vorsichtig mit einem kleinen, goldenen Schlüssel und fischte einen Anhänger heraus. “I can see from your date of birth that you were born in June. That probably makes you **Gemini**, doesn't it? Gemini – the Twins. We've got a Gemini **pendant** somewhere too. Maybe your husband would like to buy you one as a gift.”

Plötzlich spürte Laura Peters Atem hinter sich und roch sein Aftershave. Musk – er roch unglaublich sexy und flüsterte ihr zu: “Mrs Rutherford is wonderful, but she's a real *Sabbeltasche*, isn't she!”

Laura fuhr herum, als sie das deutsche Wort hörte. “How come you speak German, Peter?”

“I don't speak German that well, actually. I **picked** a bit **up** when I was working in Berlin”, erwiderte er schelmisch.

---

celebrity [sə'lebrətɪ] Prominente **Gemini** ['dʒemɪnaɪ] Zwilling **pendant** ['pendənt] Anhänger **to pick up** [ˌpɪk 'ʌp] *hier:* mitbekommen

Dann nahm er die Koffer, räusperte sich laut und schaute herausfordernd zur Rezeptionistin. Die verstand glücklicherweise den Wink, schloss die Tür der Glasvitrine sorgfältig ab und fragte höflich: "Would you like to go up to your rooms **straight away** or would you prefer to have a cup of coffee or tea first?"

Milena schüttelte erschöpft den Kopf. "Thank you, Mrs Rutherford, but I'**m dying to** see my room, and . . ."

Bevor sie ausreden konnte, wurde sie von einer laut schimpfenden Stimme unterbrochen. In einem der Gänge tauchte eine stattliche Mittfünfzigerin auf. Sie war in ein wallendes rotes Gewand gehüllt und trug eine ebenso rote Handtasche, aus der ein Chihuahua mit großen Augen herausschaute.

Die Frau lief leicht torkelnd auf eines der Tischchen zu.

"Oh dear, here's Zaphira Parsons", seufzte Mrs. Rutherford, "and she's been drinking too much again!"

Zaphira stieß an den Tisch, als sie sich ächzend auf dem Stuhl niederließ. Die Vase darauf kippte um, und das Wasser lief auf den Boden. Die Frau kümmerte sich nicht darum, aber ihr kleiner Hund begann erbärmlich zu jaulen. Mrs. Rutherford lief eilig zu einem kleinen Servierwagen, schnappte sich ein paar Servietten und wischte behände Tisch und Fußboden.

Zaphiras Blick landete auf Milena und Laura. "Who are *you*, then? Just arrived or what? I'll see you for cocktails this evening."

Dann fielen ihre kleinen leicht geröteten Augen auf Peter. "Now I remember why I came down here. Towels!"

---

straight away [ˌstreɪt əˈweɪ] sofort **to be (was, been) dying to do sth.** [biː / wɒz / biːn ˈdaɪɪŋ tə ˌduː] darauf brennen, etw. zu tun

"Towels?", fragte Mrs. Rutherford ungläubig und hielt in ihrer Aufräumarbeit inne.
"Yes, towels. Are you **deaf** or what? I need towels in my room", schnauzte Zaphira.
"But I put some there this morning. Fresh **fluffy** ones, just the way you like them." Mrs. Rutherford wirkte aufrichtig irritiert.
"**Shut up**, you idiot. You talk too much. One day somebody will shut you up for good, if you're not careful! Don't say I didn't warn you!" Zaphira stand auf und schwankte dabei gewaltig, wie ein Schiff im Sturm.
Laura drehte sich angewidert zu Milena. "Poor Mrs Rutherford. How can people be so **objectionable**?"
Milena winkte ab. "I've interviewed dozens of movie stars who have had **tantrums** ten times worse than this!"
"Is she a movie star then? I've never heard of her."
"Zaphira Parsons **is** more of a **has-been** these days. She was at the height of her **fame** about fifteen years ago. Since then she's only been able to get **bit parts**."
Zaphira zog vorsichtig eine silberne Thermosflasche aus ihrer Tasche und streichelte dabei ihren Hund. "I want Peter to bring me fresh towels and Sylvie to fill my water bottle. **Where the hell** is Sylvie?", maulte sie.
Mrs. Rutherford warf die nassen Servietten in einen kleinen Tischmülleimer. "Mrs Stone isn't here yet. Can I fill the bottle up for you?"

---

deaf [def] taub **fluffy** ['flʌfɪ] flauschig **Shut up!** ['ʃʌt ˌʌp] Halt den Mund! **objectionable** [əb'dʒekʃnəbl] taktlos **tantrum** ['tæntrəm] Wutanfall **to be (was, been) a has-been** [bi: / wɒz / bi:n ə 'hæzbi:n] weg vom Fenster sein **fame** [feɪm] Ruhm **bit part** ['bɪt pɑ:t] kleine Nebenrolle **where the hell** ['weə ðə ˌhel] wo zum Teufel

Zaphira schien nicht zu Kompromissen aufgelegt. “No, certainly not”, kreischte sie. “I want Sylvie to do it.”
Peter schaltete sich ein: “I think Mrs Stone is walking along the beach with Mr Kaden. They’re looking for Mr Stone. He’s out doing some bird-watching, I believe.”
Zaphira schnalzte und begann laut und dreckig zu lachen. “Bird-watching eh? Very funny. Bird-watching. Is that what he calls it these days?”
Laura war diese ganze Situation extrem unangenehm.
Plötzlich öffnete sich die Tür mit dem Schild ‘Diane Bragg’. Eine attraktive, junge Frau mit vollem rotem Haar schoss heraus. Ihre Haare waren allerdings zerzaust, und ihr kurzes geblümtes Kleid sah verknittert aus. “**What’s up?**”, stutzte sie. “**Oh my goodness**, Mrs Parsons! What’s wrong?” Sie zog die Tür sorgfältig hinter sich ins Schloss. “I’ll be with you right away!” Mit einem professionellen Lächeln auf den ungeschminkten Lippen eilte sie in Richtung Zaphira. Dann erst bemerkte sie die Neuankömmlinge. Für einen Augenblick schien sie nicht zu wissen, um wen sie sich zuerst kümmern sollte. Dann sagte sie entschuldigend zu Zaphira: “I’ll be with you in a second, Mrs Parsons. Just let me welcome our guests!” Und sie lief mit demselben Lächeln auf Milena und Laura zu. Zaphira ließ sich wieder auf den Stuhl sinken, die Vase kippte erneut um und Mrs. Rutherford stellte sie geduldig wieder hin. Wasser war ja glücklicherweise keines mehr darin.

What’s up? [wɒts ˈʌp] Was ist los? **Oh my goodness!** [ˈəʊ maɪ ˌgʊdnəs] Du meine Güte!

Übung 17: Sind die folgenden Aussagen richtig (✓) oder falsch (×)?

1. ☐ Both Sylvie Stone and Diane Bragg are blonde.
2. ☐ Neither Milena nor Laura has been to the island before.
3. ☐ Both Zaphira and Sylvie have acting experience.
4. ☐ Neither Mrs Rutherford nor Diane Bragg is interested in astrology.
5. ☐ Both Milena and Laura are married.
6. ☐ Neither Sylvie nor Milena is interested in astrology.
7. ☐ Both Peter Saunders and Sylvie Stone love jogging.
8. ☐ Neither Ted nor Laura has good sea-legs.

"How do you do? We weren't expecting you quite so early. But I hope you enjoy your stay here. My name is Diane Bragg. I'm Mrs Stone's P.A."
Während sie ihre Hand schüttelte, nahm Laura ihren Geruch in sich auf. Sie trug ein Parfüm mit einem Hauch Bergamotte, was nicht zu ihr zu passen schien. Doch ehe Laura in Worte fassen konnte, was ihr an Dianes Geruch seltsam vorkam, lief diese schon zu Zaphira und sprach beruhigend auf sie ein. Die alte Schauspielerin ließ sich tatsächlich von ihr beruhigen. "Come this way, Mrs Parsons. And you as well, Bouncer." Diane streichelte den Chihuahua und führte die Frau durch einen der Gänge fort.
Milena sah ihr bewundernd nach. "She's quite **a smooth operator**."
"Yes, of course", murmelte Laura so leise, dass nur Milena sie verstehen konnte. "But why did she look so **dishevelled**?

---

to be (was, been) a smooth operator [biː / wɒz / biːn ə ˈsmuːð ˌɒpəreɪtə] raffiniert vorgehen **dishevelled** [dɪˈʃevld] zerzaust

I don't think she's the type of woman who's usually careless about her **appearance**. And that perfume? **Bergamot**! Such a very unusual scent for a woman!"

Mrs. Rutherford unterbrach ihre Gedanken. "Diane is taking her back to her room to sleep off the effects of the alcohol. She says terrible things when she's **drunk**. Not that anybody ever **acknowledges** that she's been drinking. Dr Stone calls it 'a **nervous condition**'. Hah – nervous condition, my foot! Alcohol is forbidden in the spa – that's the problem. That was Bridget Pencoe's philosophy. No alcohol! No cigarettes! Certainly not any drugs!" Mrs. Rutherford seufzte. "Only pure, natural, **organic food** and drinks to **cleanse** the body and **uplift** the soul. Yes, that's what Mrs Pencoe always said, God **bless** her!"

Laura starrte die Rezeptionistin an. "Did you know Bridget Pencoe?"

"Of course! I knew her long before this spa ever opened. She always used to **catch** the ferry between Penzance and St Mary's. At that time she was still working in London as a **naturopath** – a herb woman, as I always used to call her. I was working behind the bar on the *Scillonian* at the time. She used to give me herbal teas for my poor mother, who had arthritis. My mother swore by them. Bridget and I often used to **have a chat**, friendly-like, and then one day

---

appearance [ə'pɪərəns] Aussehen **bergamot** ['bɜːgəmɒt] Bergamotte **drunk** [drʌŋk] betrunken **to acknowledge** [ək'nɒlɪdʒ] eingestehen **nervous condition** [ˌnɜːvəs kən'dɪʃn] Nervenleiden **organic food** [ɔːˌgænɪk 'fuːd] Bio-Lebensmittel **to cleanse** [klenz] reinigen **to uplift** [ʌp'lɪft] heben **to bless** [bles] segnen **to catch (caught, caught)** [kætʃ / kɔːt / kɔːt] *hier*: nehmen **naturopath** ['neɪtʃərəpæθ] Naturheilkundige **to have (had, had) a chat** ['həv / 'hæd / 'hæd ə 'tʃæt] plaudern she told me she was going to set up this health spa. She offered me twice what I was getting on the boat if I came to work here as a receptionist. I've never **regretted** it either, even though the place is a bit remote. **Halfway** to America – that's what my mother said when I told her where I'd be working."

Laura räusperte sich, um Mrs. Rutherfords Redeschwall von ihrer eigenen Mutter weg und zu ihrer, Lauras Mutter, zurück zu lenken. "What happened to Bridget?"

"Oh, that's a mystery. One day she just disappeared! Ted the **boatman** – you've met him, I believe – Ted and I **were courting.** The day Bridget left to go to Germany to meet up with her family, I went for a walk with Ted along the cliffs. It was the middle of December and pretty cold, but we were young and in love, and so what did a little cold matter! The two of us were standing near the cairn – that's that pile of rocks on top of the hill behind the spa. Well, Ted and I **were** quite **wrapped up in each other, so to speak**", sie errötete sanft, während sie von ihrer Liebschaft mit dem Bootsmann erzählte, "but we saw her get on the boat with Clive. It was a really windy day, and you could see her blonde hair **whipped** by the breeze ..." Plötzlich wirkte Mrs. Rutherford unendlich traurig. "I never saw Bridget Pencoe again."

Sie hörten Schritte, und Diane Bragg kehrte zurück. Sie blieb neben dem Rosenbusch an ihrer Tür stehen und

---

to regret [rɪ'gret] bereuen **halfway** [ˌhɑːf'weɪ] halbwegs **boatman** ['bəʊtmən] Bootsmann **to court with so** ['kɔːt wɪð] mit jmdm. gehen **to be (was, been) wrapped up in each other** [biː / wɒz / biːn ˌræpt 'ʌp ɪn iːtʃ 'ʌðə] sehr miteinander beschäftigt sein **so to speak** [səʊ tə 'spiːk] sozusagen **whipped** ['wɪpt] gepeitscht wirkte gehetzt. Haare und Kleid hatte sie allerdings wieder etwas in Ordnung gebracht, wie Laura bemerkte. "I must apologize for that little scene. I'm afraid that Mrs Parsons gets a little **over-excited** at this time of day! It's a nervous condition."

Milena hatte sich müde an einen der Tische gesetzt. "Where does she get the **booze** from, Ms Bragg? It's not allowed here, is it? I'd like to know because I might need a good strong drink myself sometime."

Doch Diane ignorierte diese Frage. "Would you like Peter to show you your rooms now? Maybe you both need a rest before we have dinner."

Laura wurde den Eindruck nicht los, Diane wolle sie möglichst schnell loswerden. Trotzdem folgte sie Milena und Peter durch den Gang bis zu einer Tür.

"This is your room, Ms Krüger. And the Kadens are here, right **next door**." Peter brachte Milenas Koffer zu ihrem Zimmer ein Stück weiter den Gang hinunter. Milena zwinkerte Laura zu. "I'm going to lie down for a minute. *Ciao bella! Ciao bello*!" Dann schloss sich ihre Tür.

Laura betrat ihr Zimmer, gefolgt von Peter, der ihren Koffer neben den Schrank stellte. "You've got a very interesting view from your window. You can see the sea and the cairn on top of the hill. It's about two thousand years old. At that time the Scillies weren't separate islands. This area was all part of a huge peninsula. When the **sea levels** rose, only the hills **remained** – as islands."

---

over-excited [ˌəʊvərɪk'saɪtɪd] überreizt **booze** [buːz] Fusel
next door [nekst 'dɔː] nebenan **sea level** ['siː ˌlevl] Meeresspiegel
to remain [rɪ'meɪn] (zurück)bleiben

"Wow", staunte Laura. "Just like the lost continent of Atlantis."

Übung 18: Fügen Sie die passende Modalverbform ein.
(mustn't, don't have to, used to, shouldn't, could, can)

1. You ________________ smoke or drink at the spa. It's forbidden.
2. Mrs Rutherford ________________ work on the *Scillonian*.
3. Laura ____________ see the cairn from her room.
4. 2000 years ago you ________________ walk from Rose island to St Mary's.
5. Zaphira ________________ drink so much. It's bad for her.
6. Laura and Milena ________________ carry their heavy suitcases up the hill.

Als Peter gegangen war, atmete sie tief durch. Seine Anwesenheit verunsicherte sie sehr, und das gefiel ihr gar nicht. Sie schüttelte den Kopf und schaute sich um. Das Zimmer war wirklich wunderschön. Durch die Verandatür und das riesige Fenster schien die Abendsonne herein und verlieh dem Raum einen goldenen Schimmer. Selbst der weiße Marmor des Kamins glitzerte golden. Mit einem Seufzer warf sie sich auf das große Himmelbett in der Mitte des Raumes; dann stand sie wieder auf und öffnete die Veran-

datür, betrachtete voller Begeisterung die in Blau gehaltene und mit vielen Pflanzen geschmückte Veranda. Laura setzte sich in einen weißen Korbsessel und ließ ihren Blick in die Ferne schweifen – auf das glitzernde Meer und über die Insel hinweg bis hin zu den Felsen. Hier hatte sie also ihre Kindheit verbracht.
Zurück im Zimmer fiel ihr Blick auf das in die Wand eingelassene Aquarium, in dem ein paar Goldfische schwammen. "Goldfish! Excellent – a sign of success and **abundance**", murmelte sie lächelnd. Aus den Augen einer Feng-Shui-Beraterin war das Zimmer ideal.
Plötzlich klopfte es. Da sie Milena oder Wolfgang erwartete, rief sie fröhlich "Come on in", und wunderte sich, als Sylvie eintrat.
"Can I come in?"
"Of course!" Laura ging Sylvie entgegen, die ihre Hände ergriff. Ohne weitere Umschweife begann sie auf Laura einzureden. "Oh Rhiannon, I feel so guilty about everything. When your father came here ten years after Bridget disappeared and asked me to buy his share of the spa I told him to **reconsider**. I reminded him that maybe one day you would be interested in coming back and doing something with it. But he was determined to sell everything. He even asked us to buy the island off him. I think he was desperate for money."
Laura nickte. "I think he had a lot of debts at the time."
Forschend schaute Sylvie Laura an. "And what about you, Rhiannon? Are you doing okay for money?"
"Fine, thanks. Anyway, it's not your fault, Sylvie. It was my father's decision."

---

abundance [ə'bʌndəns] Wohlstand **to reconsider sth.** [ˌriːkən'sɪdə] etw. erneut überdenken

Sylvie lächelte sie erleichtert an. "You're very **understanding**. I'm so glad you're back." Sylvie umarmte sie und ließ sie dann wieder allein. Das war ein sehr kurzer Besuch gewesen! Sylvie war wirklich sehr nett und besorgt, aber offenbar auch sehr beschäftigt.
Laura zog das kleine Püppchen ihrer Mutter aus der Tasche und setzte es auf das Bett. "I know you'**ll watch out for** me, Mama", flüsterte sie der Puppe zu. Es tat gut, diese Worte auszusprechen.

Seven

Als es kurz darauf erneut klopfte, war es Milena. Sie hatte sich umgezogen und sah umwerfend aus. "Let's go down to the **buffet**. Wolfgang just came back and he's totally exhausted. He'**s fast asleep** now. We're supposed to wake him up right after the buffet – he'd like to have some of the famous Ruby Rose Soup, but he'**s going to give** the buffet **a miss**."
Lachend schlenderten sie zur Lobby.
Hinter ihrem Tresen stand Mrs. Ruthford und winkte Laura zu sich. Mit hoher Stimme fiepste sie aufgeregt: "Ms Krüger, could I **have a word with** you please? It's important!"
Milena nickte Laura zu und entfernte sich in Richtung Restaurant. Sobald sie außer Sichtweite war, flüsterte die Rezeptionistin: "I know who you are!" Sie hatte das kleine

---

understanding [ˌʌndəˈstændɪŋ] verständnisvoll **to watch out for sb.** [ˌwɒtʃ ˈaʊt fə] auf jmdn. achtgeben **buffet** [ˈbʊfeɪ] Büfett **to be (was, been) fast asleep** [biː / wɒz / biːn ˌfɑːst əˈsliːp] tief schlafen **to give (gave, given) sth. a miss** [ˌɡɪv / ˌɡeɪv / ˌɡɪvn / ə ˈmɪs] etw. auslassen **to have (had, had) a word with sb.** [ˌhæv / ˌhæd / ˌhæd ə ˈwɜːd wɪð] kurz mit jmdm. sprechen

Büchlein mit den von ihr gesammelten Geburtstagsdaten in der Hand und tippte fortwährend darauf.
Laura starrte sie entgeistert an. "What do you mean?"
"When I first saw you, I thought you looked familiar. But I **couldn't** quite **place** you. Luckily, I've collected the birthdates of most of the people I've ever met in my little book. I looked up your date of birth . . . It's the same as Rhiannon Pencoe's, Bridget Pencoe's daughter!"
Triumphierend streckte sie Laura ihr Büchlein entgegen wie zum Beweis. "And you've got your mother's eyes!"
In dem Moment fiel irgendwo eine Tür ins Schloss.
Laura erschrak ebenso wie Mrs. Rutherford. "What was that?", flüsterte Mrs. Rutherford. Sie hielten den Atem an und lauschten. Aber es war nichts mehr zu hören.
Nervös flüsterte Mrs. Rutherford: "You're here to find out what happened to your mother, aren't you? Talk to Ted. He knows what happened."
Laura stutzte. Hatte Mrs. Rutherford gerade wirklich gesagt, Ted wüsste, was geschehen war? "Ted the boatman?"
Mrs. Rutherford nickte. Sie schaute sich um, und ihre Stimme war kaum mehr als ein Wispern. "A couple of days after her **disappearance**, he told me he was sure that Bridget ..." Wieder blickte sie sich um. "Ted told me he was sure that Bridget had been *murdered*!"
Mrs. Rutherford wirkte plötzlich ängstlich und unsicher. "But walls have ears. Maybe I've said too much. Go ahead and have some dinner now."
Sie verschwand hinter ihrer Stellwand, aber Laura folgte ihr

---

to place sb. [pleɪs] jmdn. unterbringen **disappearance** [ˌdɪsəˈpɪərəns] Verschwinden

aufgeregt. "Murdered? But how? Who? Did he tell the police about his **suspicions**?"
Mrs. Rutherford schüttelte den Kopf. "No, he didn't. But if you want to know more, you'll have to ask him!"

Laura verstand. Mrs. Rutherford würde nicht mehr sagen. Aufgewühlt verließ Laura den Rückzugsort der Rezeptionistin und verharrte einen Augenblick am Tresen, um sich zu beruhigen. Fred Lightfoot ging an ihr vorbei in Richtung Restaurant und würdigte sie keines Blickes. Mit hängenden Schultern folgte sie ihm.

Übung 19: Vervollständigen Sie die folgenden if-Sätze mit der richtigen Zeitform.

1. If you *(eat)* eat______ the soup, you *(lose)* will lose______ weight.

2. *(go)* ______ Laura ______ jogging with Peter, if he *(ask)* ______ her?

3. Wolfgang *(be)* ______ happy, if he *(manage to)* ______ spot a rare bird.

4. If Zaphira *(not stop)* ______ drinking so much brandy, she *(have)* ______ serious health problems.

---

suspicion [sə'spɪʃn] Verdacht

5. Laura *(get)* ____________ her horoscope done for her, if she *(ask)* ____________ Diane Bragg.

6. If Laura *(not talk)* __________ to Ted, she *(not find)* ____________ out what he knows about her mother's disappearance.

Als Laura das Restaurant schließlich erreichte, wartete Milena schon sehnsüchtig am Buffet auf sie. "Just look around! Everything's red. There's red cheese, red **berries**, red ***hors d'oeuvres***, red grapes, red ham. It's incredible!"
Aber Laura hatte keine Augen für die angerichteten Speisen. "Milena, I have to speak to you soon – in private!"
Ein junger Kellner stand hilfsbereit neben dem Büffet. "Would you like to try one of Jean-Paul's special fruit cocktails? They're all red, too. We have Berry Root, Pink Lady, Rhapsody in Red, Sunset on the Beach, . . ."
Milena griff sich zwei knallrote Berry Roots und reichte Laura einen davon. "Let's try this one." Leise fügte sie hinzu: "Don't worry! We'll sneak off in a minute! Let's just get something to eat first."
Milena konnte vermutlich immer essen; Laura hingegen war der Appetit gründlich vergangen. Aber sie probierte den Saft. "Not as bad as it looks."
Laura ließ ihren Blick durch den Raum wandern. Nicht nur das Essen, alles in diesem Raum war rot. Schwere weinrote Vorhänge hingen neben der Terrassentür und ergänzten sich gut mit den blassrosafarbenen Tapeten. In der Mitte

---

berry ['berɪ] Beere **hors d'oeuvre** [ɔː 'dɜːv] Vorspeise des Raumes harrte eine lange Tafel samt roter Tischdecke mit Rosenmuster ihrer Gäste. Die glutroten Kerzen in den drei schweren silbernen Kerzenleuchtern waren nicht angezündet; die restlichen Tische des Speisesaals waren an die Wand geschoben worden. Laura erinnerte sich daran, dass Wolfgang ihr erzählt hatte, dass das Hotel zurzeit eigentlich geschlossen war und sie sich nur mit wenigen ausgewählten Gästen hier befand – mit Milena und Wolfgang, Zaphira und diesem seltsamen Fred Lightfoot, der an einem Ende der Tafel saß und bereits rote Häppchen aß. Darüber hinaus gab es hier zurzeit scheinbar nur noch die Bediensteten des Hauses.

Laura setzte sich mit Milena ans andere Ende des Tisches. Da betrat Zaphira Parsons den Raum. Sie wirkte nun ruhiger, und der kleine Hund in ihrer übergroßen Tasche schien zu schlafen. Zaphira steuerte geradewegs auf den Kellner zu. "Which cocktail can you recommend today, David?" Sie flatterte mit den Augenlidern und strahlte den um Jahrzehnte jüngeren David kokett an.

Laura und Milena wechselten ungläubige Blicke.

"Well, Mrs Parsons, this lady here", David zeigte augenzwinkernd auf Laura, "has just **unreservedly** recommended our raspberry **beetroot** combination called Berry Root. Would you like to try it, perhaps? Or would you prefer a Raspberry Rapture?"

Zaphira kicherte wie ein Backfisch. "Rapture, please, David. Give me rapture any time!"

David errötete, gab ihr aber den gewünschten Cocktail, und sie sog den Saft durch den Strohhalm. Dann kraulte sie

---

unreservedly [ˌʌnrɪˈzɜːvədlɪ] uneingeschränkt **beetroot** [ˈbiːtruːt] Rote Beete

den armen Kellner am Kinn. "Oh, David, has anyone ever told you that you're **cute**! I mean, *really* cute!"
David lächelte diskret, murmelte ein "Excuse me" und verschwand in der Küche.
Mit einem Achselzucken machte sich Zaphira Cocktail schlürfend über das Büffet her. Ohne zu fragen, setzte sie sich dann mit ihrem Teller neben Laura. "Isn't that man cute? David invited me to his birthday party last May. I couldn't make it because I was filming a **commercial**. He was just **heartbroken**, poor thing!" Sie musterte Laura kritisch. "So what do you do, darling? Are you **in modelling** or something?"
"Actually, I'm an interior designer, and occasionally I do feng shui, too", antwortete Laura gedehnt, während Milena an einem roten *hors d'oeuvre* in Streichholzformat knabberte.
Zaphira runzelte die Stirn. "Feng shui? What the hell is that? Japanese?"
Laura räusperte sich. Zaphira war dumm und arrogant, eine sehr ungesunde Kombination, wie Laura fand. "Feng shui is an ancient spiritual discipline from *China*, not Japan. In diesem Moment kam Sylvie in einem grasgrünen Kostüm aus der Küche, an ihrer Seite ein älterer Mann mit Kochmütze. Fröhlich begrüßte sie ihre wenigen Gäste. "I hope you're enjoying the buffet. I'd like to introduce you to our chef, Jean-Paul. He's the one who **came up with** all the ideas."

---

cute [kjuːt] süß **commercial** [kəˈmɜːʃl] Werbespot **heartbroken** [ˈhɑːtˌbrəʊkən] untröstlich **Are you in modelling?** [ɑː juː ɪn ˈmodelɪŋ] Arbeiten Sie als Model? **to come (came, come) up with sth.** [ˌkʌm / ˌkeɪm / ˌkʌm ˈʌp wɪð] sich etw. ausdenken

Milena klatschte begeistert und Jean-Paul verbeugte sich. "Welcome, Ladies and ...", sein Blick fiel auf Fred Lightfoot, und er verzog für den Bruchteil einer Sekunde das Gesicht, dann lächelte er wieder – "Ladies and Gentlemen. The spa rule is – you can eat anything you like and as much as you like, as long as it's red. Red food helps you lose weight." Er hatte definitiv einen französischen Akzent.
Milena untersuchte ihre Häppchen. "This looks like a pink marshmallow. And it's as light as a **feather**."
"It's a **miniature** egg-and-beetroot soufflé, actually", erklärte Jean-Paul höflich.

Übung 20: Welche Wörter passen inhaltlich in den folgenden Vergleichen zusammen?

1. as light as	☐	**a.**	gold
2. as black as	☐	**b.**	a knife
3. as good as	☐	**c.**	a picture
4. as sharp as	☐	**d.**	the hills
5. as old as	☐	**e.**	a feather
6. as straight as	☐	**f.**	night
7. as pretty as	☐	**g.**	an arrow

Die Tür des Restaurants flog auf und Diane Bragg trat ein. Auch sie hatte sich geradezu festlich gekleidet. Ihr langes, rotes Kleid betonte ihre zarte Figur und war perfekt auf Raum und Essen abgestimmt. Laura knabberte nachdenklich an ihrem Strohhalm. Ob Peter wohl auch mit Diane so flirtete wie mit ihr? Und warum nur hatte sie selbst völlig vergessen, sich umzuziehen? Sie trug noch immer ihren hellblauen Hosenanzug, der von der Reise etwas zerknittert

---

feather ['feðə] Feder **miniature** ['mɪnətʃə] Miniaturwar. Insgeheim hoffte sie, dass Peter nicht zum Essen erscheinen würde.

Jean-Paul ließ sich von Diane Bragg, die sich neben Milena niederließ, nicht ablenken. "You'll notice how small all the portions are. But, as you'll see, they are surprisingly filling." Diane lächelte. "Jean-Paul is a real artist!"

Komplimente schien er allerdings nicht zu mögen, denn er verbeugte sich elegant und verschwand in seiner Küche. Diane fuhr ungefragt fort: "He's been working here for nearly thirty years. He's not very well, though. His heart, you know. I guess he'll retire as soon as ..." Sie hielt inne, lächelte entschuldigend und räusperte sich umständlich.

As soon as the place is sold, beendete Laura im Geiste ihren Satz.

Diane aber sagte: "Well, at least we have David to help him out."

Plötzlich kam Laura Dr. Stone in den Sinn. Wo war er eigentlich? Sie hatten ihn überhaupt noch nicht zu Gesicht bekommen. Hatten Wolfgang und Sylvie ihn am Strand getroffen? Apropos Wolfgang. Sollten sie ihn nicht bald wecken?

Milena schob immer noch ein Häppchen nach dem anderen in den Mund. Offenbar liebte sie Büffets. "Does Jean-Paul make the Ruby Rose Soup, too?", fragte sie gerade Diane.

"No, Mrs Stone and Dr Stone insist on making the soup themselves. The recipe is a secret, you know."

Sylvie hatte sich einen Cocktail genommen und gesellte sich zu ihnen. "Jean-Paul really is a genius", schwärmte sie. "Now and then I really miss France."

"Are you originally from France, then?".

Zaphira kam Sylvie zuvor. "Ah, France! Sylvie and I met in

France. She was working in an acting **troupe** that toured all over France . . . Oh, those were the days. Do you remember, Sylvie? That was just before you got your big role as Mademoiselle Lafleur – the **deadly** blonde!"
Plötzlich jaulte Bouncer laut auf. Der junge Kellner David war an den Tisch getreten und versehentlich mit dem Fuß gegen die Tasche gestoßen.
"You **clumsy oaf**!", brüllte Zaphira. David entschuldigte sich und wollte Bouncer beruhigen, aber Zaphira schubste ihn weg und nahm den winselnden Hund aus der Tasche. "There, there. **Did** that clumsy waiter **tread on** my poopsie-kins? Mumsie's going to get poopsie-kins a **treat**." Sie ging zum Büffet und schob dem Kleinen ein paar Häppchen in die Schnauze. "Have some crimson beef **tartare**, poopsie!" Gierig verschlang Bouncer alles, was sie ihm gab.
Sylvie nutzte die Gelegenheit und verschwand kopfschüttelnd in der Küche. Fred Lightfoot war aufgestanden und gesellte sich zu Lauras Überraschung zu ihnen. "Well, ladies, this is a **cosy** little group. Let's find out a bit more about each other. Shall I **start the ball rolling**?" Er begutachtete Laura. "You're a feng shui expert, I hear. What is your **star sign**?"
Zaphira, die mit Bouncer auf dem Arm vom Büffet zurückkehrte, rief lautstark: "I'm a Gemini!"

---

troupe [tru:p] Truppe **deadly** ['dedlɪ] tödlich **clumsy** ['klʌmsɪ] unbeholfen **oaf** [əʊf] Ochse **to tread (trod, trodden) on sth.** ['tred / 'trɒd / 'trɒdn ɒn] auf etw. treten **treat** [tri:t] Leckerei **tartare** ['tɑ:tə] Tatar **cosy** ['kəʊzɪ] gemütlich **to start the ball rolling** [ˌstɑ:t ðə bɔ:l 'rəʊlɪŋ] den Anfang machen **star sign** ['stɑ: saɪn] Sternzeichen

"Oh, that's funny", sagte Milena und lächelte. "We're twins! I'm a Gemini, too."
Diane Bragg schaute die beiden interessiert an. "Geminis are **seekers** of knowledge."
Zaphira zuckte die Achseln und musterte Laura. "And what sign are you, then?"
Laura zögerte. "I'm a **Virgo**. Are Virgos seekers of knowledge too, Ms Bragg?"
"No", Diane winkte ab. "Knowledge isn't enough for Virgos. They want more than that. Much more. Virgos are seekers of the truth."
Für einen Augenblick ruhten die Augen der Anwesenden auf Laura. Fred Lightfoot räusperte sich. "I was born between two signs – **Cancer** and **Leo**. My dear mother can't remember the exact time."
Diane zog eine ihrer akkurat gezupften Augenbrauen in die Höhe: "Oh, so you **were born on the cusp**."
Aber Fred ignorierte sie und wandte sich erneut Laura und Milena zu.

Übung 21: Vervollständigen Sie mit der richtigen Zeitform (Present Progressive, Present Simple, Past Simple or Present Perfect).

"And where **1.** ______________ you *(live)* ______________, ladies? My spiritual home is close to nature, side by side with my brothers, the Great Sioux Indians." Dann fügte er

---

seeker ['si:kə] Sucher **Virgo** ['vɜ:gəʊ] Jungfrau **Cancer** ['kænsə] Krebs **Leo** ['li:əʊ] Löwe **to be (was, been) born on the cusp** [bi: / wɒz / bi:n 'bɔ:n ɒn ðə 'kʌsp] zwischen zwei Sternzeichen geboren sein

kleinlaut hinzu: "But I **2.** *(stay)* ______________________
with friends in Birmingham at the moment."
"And I **3.** *(live)* ______________________ in Hamburg. I **4.** *(stay)* ______________________ here for a couple of days", erwiderte Laura und empfand zum ersten Mal ein kleines bisschen Sympathie für diesen seltsamen Mann.

Milena nickte. "Me too. Originally I'm from New York, but I **5.** *(just move)* ________________ to Hamburg with my husband."

Zaphiras Stirn legte sich in tiefe Falten. "Hamburg! Hamburg? I once knew someone who **6.** *(live)* ______________ in Hamburg a long time ago, but I don't remember who!"

Fragend sah Milena sie an. "**7.** __________ you *(ever hear)* ______________ of Bridget Pencoe for example?"

"Bridget Pencoe? Yes, of course. And her husband Malcolm **8.** *(be)* ______________ from Hamburg."

"Martin!", korrigierte Laura wie aus der Pistole geschossen und ärgerte sich im gleichen Moment über ihre Unachtsamkeit. Sie sog intensiv an ihrem Strohhalm.
Aber Zaphira war noch zu sehr damit beschäftigt, sich ihr vom Alkohol strapaziertes Hirn zu zermartern. Plötzlich

rief sie: "Bridget Pencoe! She made such wonderful face-creams! It's a shame no one ever found her recipe book when she ran off with her lover!"
Laura verschluckte sich fast. "Ran off? A lover? What do you mean?"
"Well, of course there was another man in her life apart from her husband!" Da niemand sie hinderte, redete Zaphira weiter. "What do you expect? Her husband was a sailor, after all. He was always away at sea." Sie lachte. "He probably had a girl in every port!"
Milena warf Laura einen beschwörenden Blick zu und fragte Zaphira: "But can you be certain? I mean, how did you know that she had a lover?"
"Women's intuition, darling. You can't beat it! Believe me! I'm a woman, and I know!"
Laura kochte vor Wut. Diese Frau war nicht auszuhalten. Sie sprang auf und ging zum Büffet, obwohl sie nach wie vor keinen Hunger hatte. Doch Zaphira redete munter weiter, laut genug, dass Laura alles verstehen konnte. "I remember the day she left very well, because I had a bad case of **food poisoning**, as did Sylvie. Jean-Paul was new in those days. He was probably still trying to **get the hang of** everything."
Sie und Sylvie hatten am Tag des Verschwindens ihrer Mutter eine Lebensmittelvergiftung gehabt? Laura hielt inne. Vielleicht war ihre Mutter daran gestorben? Aber dann hätte die Polizei sie sicherlich irgendwo gefunden . . .
Zaphira blubberte derweil weiter. "Anyway, as I said to the

---

food poisoning ['fuːd ˌpɔɪznɪŋ] Lebensmittelvergiftung **to get (got, got) the hang of sth.** [ˌget / ˌgɒt / ˌgɒt ðə 'hæŋ əv] mit etw. umzugehen lernen police when they sent that funny inspector here to investigate what had happened, I was standing near the front door when Clive and Bridget left. I said goodbye to Bridget and wished her all the best for Christmas. I watched her and Clive walk down the steps and get onto the boat. You have a good view of the **jetty** from the path. The regular boatman – Tim, Ted, Tom or something – hadn't turned up for work that day. I think he had a girlfriend, someone who worked in the hotel. They **were** probably **fooling around** with each other somewhere. Well anyway, Bridget Pencoe left to meet up with her lover. I'm certain of that. It's what I've always said. **No skin off my nose** anyway. Just a shame about the face creams." Sie hielt inne, und ihre Stimme klang plötzlich traurig. "Shame about the sweet little **toddler**, though. Bridget's daughter. What was her name? Rhianna – some strange Celtic name. She was a sweet little thing. I sometimes used to read her goodnight stories and play dolls with her. I've always wondered **what became of her.** I always wanted to have children of my own some day. I always thought I would. But now it's too late." Zaphira hatte sich in eine Art dramatische Szene hineingesteigert. Allerdings schien sie sich selbst zu glauben. Sie schneuzte laut in ein Taschentuch, das Diane ihr gereicht hatte. "Anyway, there's **no use crying over spilt milk,** is there. What's done is done! Excuse me for a moment, will you. I just need to get a breath of fresh air!" Aus der Tasche zog

---

jetty ['dʒetɪ] Landeplatz **to fool around** [ˌfuːl əˈraʊnd] herumalbern **No skin off my nose.** [nəʊ 'skɪn ɒf maɪ ˌnəʊz] Das juckt mich nicht. **toddler** ['tɒdlə] Kleinkind **What became of her?** [wɒt bɪ'keɪm əv ˌhɜː] Was ist aus ihr geworden? **No use crying over spilt milk.** [nəʊ juːz 'kraɪɪŋ əʊvə ˌspɪlt 'mɪlk] Was passiert ist, ist passiert.

sie die silberne Thermoskanne heraus und verschwand damit durch die Tür. Laura nutzte die Gelegenheit, um an den Tisch zurückzukehren.
Fred Lightfoot beugte sich zu ihr und murmelte: "Don't pay any attention to her. I know what I'm talking about because I had a similar problem many years ago with cocaine! I managed to **overcome** it eventually. Mrs Parsons' problem is that she drinks too much brandy!"
Laura starrte Fred an und musste plötzlich an den Reim denken, von dem Wolfgang ihnen auf dem Schiff erzählt hatte. Wie ging er noch?
Brandy for the parson, baccy for the clerk. . .
Brandy for the parson – brandy for Mrs Parsons.
Seufzend griff sie erneut nach ihrem Cocktail.

Nine

"The famous Ruby Rose Soup is nearly ready!" Mit diesen Worten kam Sylvie freudestrahlend aus der Küche zurück.
Milena stand auf. "Then I'd better go and get Wolfgang.
Laura sprang auf und folgte ihr. "I'm just going to the ladies", murmelte sie. Milena und Laura liefen durch den Gang und verschwanden in der Damentoilette. Als sie sich versichert hatten, dass sie wirklich allein waren, flüsterte Laura: "Mrs Rutherford used to be Ted's girlfriend, and the two of them were watching as Clive took my mother to St Mary's. But Mrs Rutherford told me something else, too. She told me that Ted thinks that my mother was . . . murdered."

---

to overcome (overcame, overcome) sth. [ˌəʊvəˈkʌm / ˌəʊvəˈkeɪm / ˌəʊvəˈkʌm] etw. überwinden

“What? Murdered? Did she say who did it?”
“No, but it has to be Clive, doesn’t it?”
“But that doesn’t make any sense. The police found some **witnesses** who said that a woman matching her description was seen on the *Scillonian*, and Clive wasn’t there with her. Maybe this mysterious lover, if he existed – which I doubt – killed her somewhere on the mainland.”
Der ‘mysteriöse Liebhaber’ verursachte Laura Übelkeit, aber sie schob den Gedanken energisch beiseite. “I don’t think that’s likely. Anyway, Mrs Rutherford said that I should talk to Ted.”
“But when will he be back again?”, seufzte Milena, während sie sich im Spiegel betrachtete. “Especially if the weather gets stormy.”
Plötzlich wurde die Tür aufgerissen; es war Sylvie. “Milena dear, there you are”, säuselte sie. Laura und Milena waren zusammengezuckt wie zwei Schulmädchen. “Wolfgang has already arrived. Everyone is waiting for you. Please hurry up before the soup gets cold.”
“We’ll be right there”, versprach Laura.
Sylvie nickte und verschwand wieder. Verstohlen sahen sie einander an. Hatte Sylvie ihr Gespräch belauscht?
Eilig kehrten sie zum Restaurant zurück.

Übung 22: Unterstreichen Sie die richtige Zeitform: Past Simple oder Past Continuous?

1. Jean-Paul *(tried/was trying)* to get the hang of cooking when he first *(started/was starting)* work at the spa.
2. Zaphira *(met/was meeting)* Sylvie in France where Sylvie *(worked/was working)* in an acting troupe.

---

witness [ˈwɪtnəs] Zeuge

3. While Zaphira and Sylvie *(talked/were talking)* David *(stepped/was stepping)* on Bouncer.
4. Milena *(lived/was living)* in New York when she first *(met/was meeting)* Wolfgang.
5. When Martin *(fell/was falling)* in love with Bridget, he and Wolfgang *(toured/were touring)* the Scillies.

Die Kerzen in den Silberlüstern waren angezündet worden und tauchten den Raum jetzt in ein sanftes Licht. Die Tafel war gedeckt mit Silberbesteck und filigranen, weißen Untertellern mit Rosenmuster. Über den Himmel zogen mittlerweile dunkle Wolken; das Unwetter würde vermutlich nicht mehr lange auf sich warten lassen. Wolfgang hatte sich Fred Lightfoot gegenüber gesetzt, und an seiner Seite thronte Zaphira. Als Milena und Laura eintraten, stand Wolfgang auf.
"Oh, what a gentleman!", kicherte die Schauspieldiva. Milena kümmerte sich nicht darum und küsste ihren Mann innig. Laura hörte sie flüstern: "Hi there, **sleepyhead**. Awake at last."
Milena setzte sich neben ihren Mann, und Laura wählte den Platz ihr gegenüber. Sylvie stand am Kopfende des Tisches. Am anderen Ende der Tafel war noch ein freier Platz, und Sylvie deutete entschuldigend darauf. "My husband Clive will be down shortly. He said we could go ahead and start."
Sie setzte sich und seufzte. "Isn't this cosy? Normally all the tables are full. I love this time of the year when we just have friends here."
Die Tür zum Speisesaal flog auf, und ein dunkelhaariger

---

sleepyhead ['sliːpɪhed] Schlafmütze

gutaussehender Mittfünfziger stürmte herein. “Good evening, everybody. I’m afraid I’ve got some bad news. There’s going to be a bad storm tomorrow, and we’ll probably be cut off from the mainland for a couple of days”, verkündete er.
Sylvie erhob sich wieder und lächelte. “May I introduce this **bearer** of bad news – my husband, Dr Clive Stone!”
Die Begrüßungszeremonie wurde unterbrochen durch Jean-Paul und David, die jetzt mit Tabletts voller Porzellanschalen hereinkamen und die sehnlich erwartete Speise verteilten. Milena begutachtete die Suppe genau. “**Well, well.** So this is the famous Ruby Rose Soup. Finally! Wow, look at those tiny, pink rose **petals floating** on top! It smells **heavenly.**”
Sylvie strahlte. “You may eat as many portions as you like. We recommend **seasoning** it with **sea-salt** and pepper. The **grinders** are in front of you.”
Die Suppe schmeckte Laura ausgezeichnet, auch wenn sie, wie alle anderen, nachwürzte. Weder Sylvie noch Clive schien das etwas auszumachen. Laura selbst war da etwas pingeliger. Wenn sie für Bekannte kochte, dann empfand sie es als eine Beleidigung, wenn jemand nachwürzte.
Fred Lightfoot leckte sich die Lippen und ließ sich eine weitere Portion bringen. “This soup is so spiritual. I can feel it cleaning my cells.”
Auch Wolfgang seufzte zufrieden. “Well, Miss Sylvie, the soup tastes better than ever.”

---

bearer ['beərə] Überbringer **Well, well.** [wel 'wel] So, so! **petal** ['petl] Blütenblatt **to float** [fləʊt] schwimmen **heavenly** ['hevnlɪ] himmlisch **to season** ['siːzn] würzen **sea-salt** ['siːsɔːlt] Meeressalz **grinder** ['graɪndə] Mühle

Sylvie kicherte. "Well, my dear Wolfgang, I try my very best!"
Dann wurde sie ernst. "But really it's Bridget Pencoe that we have to thank." Sylvies Augen wanderten zu einem Portrait über dem Kamin. Laura verschluckte sich fast an der Suppe. Es zeigte eine Frau, die aus einem Fenster auf das Meer blickte. Das Fenster, die Aussicht – es war das Zimmer, in das Laura gerade eingezogen war! Und die Frau auf dem Bild war – ihre Mutter!
Clive, der seine Suppe noch nicht angerührt hatte, erklärte: "That's Bridget Pencoe, our old business partner. She's looking out of the window of her room here at the Ruby Rose Spa. It was painted a few months before she disappeared."
Plötzlich sprang Sylvie auf. "Oh, Clive. We haven't had a chance to talk since I got back. This is Wolfgang's wife Milena – and this", sie deutete auf Laura, "is Rhiannon Laura Pencoe."
Clive schnappte nach Luft, fing sich dann aber wieder. Er stand auf, um Laura händeschüttelnd zu begrüßen. Dabei inspizierte er sie wie ein seltenes Insekt. "Rhiannon Laura Pencoe? But that's impossible! Bridget's daughter?"
Und da war er wieder, dieser Geruch von Bergamotte. Lauras Blick wanderte von Diane zu Dr. Clive Stone, und dann wusste sie es. Clive betrog seine Frau. Mit Diane Bragg.
Zaphira fand als erste ihre Sprache wieder: "You are little Rhiannon Pencoe?"
Laura nickte. "Yes, I came here to find out what happened to my mother. I came here to find out the truth."
Sie hielt inne. Alle Augen waren auf sie gerichtet. Zaphira nahm einen großen Schluck aus ihrer Thermosflasche.
Laura schaute nacheinander Sylvie, Clive, Diane, Fred und Zaphira an. Vielleicht war der Mörder oder die Mörderin

unter ihnen? Diane war die einzige, die nicht in Frage kam; aber vielleicht wusste sie etwas? Jetzt erblickte Laura auch Jean-Paul, der mit einem weiteren vollen Tablett und leicht geöffnetem Mund in der Tür zur Küche stand. Auch er war damals schon hier gewesen. Theoretisch hätte also auch er . . .
Plötzlich stieß Zaphira einen spitzen Schrei aus und stand auf. "Oh my God! Rhiannon! Bridget's daughter. I don't believe it. God wants to punish me!" Sie schwankte zur Tür. Bouncer kläffte hinter ihr her, aber Zaphira achtete nicht darauf.
"Wait, Zaphira, wait!", rief Sylvie ihr hinterher, aber Clive bremste sie.
"Leave her, Sylvie. You know what she's like when she has one of her **turns**." Er lächelte die Gäste beruhigend an. "Zaphira suffers from a nervous condition. You never know what mood she's going to be in. Tomorrow she'**ll be as right as rain.**"
Milena, die bereits die zweite Schale Suppe löffelte, tat, als sei nichts weiter geschehen. "Oh, I nearly forgot! As I told your wife earlier, I've heard a rumour that you're going to sell this place? Is that true?"
Clive hatte sich scheinbar wieder im Griff; er lächelte gezwungen und schaute seine Frau fragend an.
Diane war zusammengezuckt, das hatte Laura genau gesehen. Was wusste sie von den Verkaufsplänen? Was hatte sie damit zu tun?
Clive räusperte sich. "Well, it's very exhausting working here . . ."
Seine Frau unterbrach ihn und sprach freudestrahlend

---

turn [tɜːn] *hier:* Anfall **to be (was, been) as right as rain** [biː / wɒz / biːn əz ˌraɪt əz ˈreɪn] in Ordnung sein weiter. " . . . and Clive and I simply don't have enough time for each other. It was a **heartrending** decision, but we'**ve made up our minds.** We're going to sell the spa and move to Australia." Begeistert sah sie in die Runde, doch niemand der Anwesenden schien ihre Freude zu teilen. Jean-Paul verschwand wieder in der Küche. Noch ehe jemand reagieren konnte, öffnete sich die Tür erneut, und Peter trat in Begleitung einer älteren Dame ein. Mit gemischten Gefühlen stellte Laura fest, dass sie sich freute, ihn zu sehen.

Peter geleitete die Frau zur Tafel und stellte sie Milena und Laura vor. "Ladies, this is Helga Swenson, the best **masseuse** this side of Sweden. Helga, this is Ms Krüger from Germany and Mrs Kaden from New York."

Übung 23: Fügen Sie die Gefühlswörter ein.
*(determined, offended, enjoyed, pleased, shocked, **suspicious**)*

1. Zaphira is ______________ to find out that Laura is Bridget's daughter.

2. Laura is ______________ to find out what happened to her mother.

3. Laura is ______________ about Clive and Diane.

---

heartrending [ˈhɑːtˌrendɪŋ] herzzerreißend **to make (made, made) up one's mind** [ˌmeɪk / ˌmeɪd / ˌmeɪd ʌp wʌnz ˈmaɪnd] sich entscheiden für etw. **masseuse** [mæˈsɜːz] Masseurin **suspicious** [səˈspɪʃəs] argwöhnisch

4. Laura is ______________________ when her guests add extra seasoning to meals she has prepared for them.

5. Wolfgang ______________________ the taste of the soup.

6. Nobody seemed ______________________ to hear Sylvie's news.

"Sorry, Peter", korrigierte Laura ihn selbstbewusst, "but my full name is Rhiannon Laura Pencoe-Krüger."
Peter zuckte mit den Achseln und lächelte entschuldigend. "Fine, Helga, this is Ms Pencoe-Krüger." Er hatte dem Namen keinerlei Bedeutung zugemessen, aber Helga starrte sie an wie einen Geist. "Rhiannon? Is it really true?"
Peter hatte Helga einen Stuhl hingeschoben, und die grauhaarige Frau sank dankbar darauf, ihren Blick noch immer auf Laura gerichtet.
"So you knew my mother?", fragte Laura und wischte sich mit ihrer Rosenserviette die Mundwinkel ab.
"Did I know your mother?", erwiderte Helga entrüstet. "Of course I knew her. She spent hours trying to teach me English. I'm Swedish, you know, and when I first came to England my English was terrible. I've still got quite a **thick** accent. Sometimes Sylvie **imitates** my accent and **has** us all **in stitches.**"
Laura hörte den schwedischen Akzent. Ihr Blick fiel auf

---

thick [θɪk] breit **to imitate sb.** [ˈɪmɪteɪt] jmdn. nachahmen
to have (had, had) sb. in stitches [hæv / hæd / hæd / ɪn ˈstɪtʃəs] jmdn. aus vollem Herzen zum Lachen bringen

Peter, dessen warme Augen auf ihr ruhten. Er schien jetzt verstanden zu haben, worum es hier ging.
"It's so tragic that Bridget's gone", flüsterte Sylvie.
Helga Swenson schaute Laura immer noch an. "Your mother was an angel. You look just like her!" Wie in einem schlechten Film grollte in diesem Augenblick ein Donner in der Ferne, und alle zuckten zusammen.
Milena ergriff die Initiative und erhob sich. "I hope you don't mind, but I'd love to go for a short walk before the storm starts."
"And who's going jogging with Peter and me tomorrow morning at seven, **weather permitting**?", fragte Sylvie.
Laura schüttelte den Kopf und glaubte Enttäuschung in Peters Augen zu erkennen. Sie lächelte ihm entschuldigend zu. "Seven o'clock is too early for me, but I'**ll keep** Milena **company** now." Sie stand auf. "I'd love to get some fresh air before going to bed."

Während die Gesellschaft sich auflöste, verkündete Sylvie: "I'm just **going to check on** the plants in the garden." Und eilig verließ sie den Raum, gefolgt von ihrem Mann.
Helga legte ihren Arm um Laura und raunte ihr zu: "Your mother used to write me letters, mainly to help me with my English. If you like, I can look for them. Would you like to read them?"
"Oh, thank you, Helga! I'd love to." Laura war gerührt. Sie würde Briefe ihrer Mutter zu lesen bekommen!

---

weather permitting ['weðə pə'mɪtɪŋ] wenn es das Wetter erlaubt
to keep (kept, kept) sb. company [kiːp / kept / kept / 'kʌmpənɪ] jmdm. Gesellschaft leisten **to check on sth.** ['tʃek ɒn] etw. kontrollieren

"Good night, and sleep well, Laura. I'm looking forward to talking to you some more in the morning." Mit diesen Worten verließ auch Helga, langsam und vorsichtig, das Restaurant.

Milena stuppste Laura im Vorbeigehen an. "Give me ten minutes to change and I'll meet you in the lobby."

Laura schlenderte hinter den anderen her. Sie hatte noch immer keine Lust, sich umzuziehen.

Plötzlich hörte sie Peters Stimme hinter sich. "I just wanted to say ... "

Sie fuhr herum und er hielt inne.

"Yes?"

"I just wanted to say that if you need any help, let me know, okay?"

Gegen das Lächeln, das sich langsam in ihrem Gesicht ausbreitete, war nichts auszurichten. Sie sah ihre Felle im Kampf gegen das aufbrandende Gefühl des Verliebtseins davontreiben. Am liebsten wäre sie in seine Arme gesunken. Stattdessen nickte sie nur barsch, drehte sich dann schnell wieder um und lief, an Fred Lightfoot vorbei, den langen Flur hinab.

Ten

Laura wartete in der Empfangshalle auf Milena. Mrs. Rutherford war nicht zu sehen; Laura rief nach ihr, aber niemand antwortete. Auf dem Tresen lag das kleine Buch mit den Geburtsdaten. Ob wohl etwas über ihre Mutter darin stand? Kurz rang Laura mit sich, dann schlug sie es auf.

Am Anfang des Buchs waren alle Sternzeichen und die dazu gehörigen Symbole fein säuberlich aufgelistet: Aries –

The **Ram**, **Taurus** – The **Bull**, Gemini – The Twins, Cancer – The **Crab**, Leo – The **Lion**, Virgo – The **Virgin**, **Libra** – The **Scales**, **Scorpio** – The **Scorpion**, **Sagittarius** – The **Archer**, **Capricorn** – The **Mountain Goat**, **Aquarius** – The Water Bearer, **Pisces** – The Fishes.

Laura wollte weiterblättern, als ein schriller Schrei sie zusammenzucken ließ. Er kam aus dem Zimmer von Sylvie und Clive. Es war eindeutig Sylvies Stimme, die sie jetzt hörte. "I don't want to know, Clive . . ." Dann wurde ihre Stimme leiser, sodass Laura nichts weiter verstehen konnte, auch nicht eine eventuelle Antwort Clives. "But we can't turn back the clock!" Das war wieder deutlich zu vernehmen.

Arme Sylvie. Ob Clive ihr seine Affäre gebeichtet hatte? Zum Glück kam Milena in diesem Augenblick den Gang herunter gelaufen, und Laura zog sie erleichtert mit sich nach draußen.

Übung 24: Was bedeuten diese Redewendungen? Kreuzen Sie an.

1. We can't turn back the clock.
- **a.** ☐ We can't change what we did in the past.
- **b.** ☐ We can't forget what we did in the past.

2. She had us in stitches.
- **a.** ☐ She said something insulting.
- **b.** ☐ She said something funny.

Ram [ræm] Widder **Taurus/Bull** ['tɔ:rəs / bʊl] Stier **Crab** [kræb] Krebs **Lion** ['laɪən] Löwe **Virgin** ['vɜ:dʒɪn] Jungfrau **Libra/Scales** ['li:brə / 'skeɪlz] Waage **Scorpio/Scorpion** ['skɔ:pɪəʊ / 'skɔ:pɪən] Skorpion **Sagittarius** [ˌsædʒɪ'teərɪəs] Schütze **archer** ['ɑ:tʃə] Bogenschütze **Capricorn/Mountain goat** ['kæprɪkɔ:n / 'maʊntɪn gəʊt] Steinbock **Aquarius** [ə'kweərɪəs] Wassermann **Pisces** ['paɪsi:z] Fische (Sternzeichen)

3. She'll be as right as rain.
   a. ☐ She'll be fine.
   b. ☐ She'll be drunk.
4. There's no use crying over spilt milk.
   a. ☐ There's no point in getting upset.
   b. ☐ There's no point in trying again.
5. He got the hang of it.
   a. ☐ He learned how to stop it.
   b. ☐ He learned how to do it.

Es wehte ein starker Wind und es war eindeutig, dass der Sturm nicht mehr lange auf sich warten lassen würde.
Sie liefen los, in Richtung der Steine, die Laura von ihrem Fenster aus sehen konnte. Als sie angekommen waren, ließ Laura ihre Finger über das raue Gestein gleiten. Erinnerungen und Gefühle tauchten in ihr auf, die sie nicht hätte beschreiben können.
"I wonder how many people have touched these stones over the centuries! They make you realize how short human lives are", philosophierte Milena.
"I wonder if my mother ever took me up here."
"Hush!" Milena deutete auf eine Gestalt auf dem Hügel. Es war Fred Lightfoot, in Meditation versunken.
"What a great place to meditate!", flüsterte Laura. Langsam schlenderten sie den Weg zum Hotel zurück an den Klippen entlang und schauten auf das immer wilder tobende Meer. "White horses", kicherte Milena. Dann wurde sie ernst und blieb stehen. "I don't like Clive. I can't explain why."
Laura stimmte ihr zu. "Me neither. Sylvie believes that he really is going to take her to Australia. But he's obviously interested in somebody else altogether."

Milena starrte sie neugierig an. "Do you mean Diane Bragg?"
Laura nickte. "I recognized the smell of Clive's aftershave at supper tonight. It's the same scent that I smelled on Diane when we first met her. Bergamot. Remember how dishevelled she looked when she came out of her office?"
Milenas Augen funkelten. "You mean – she and Clive had just been making love? Right there, in her office . . . "
Zögernd nickte Laura. "Yes, remember how untidy her hair was and how carefully she closed the door behind her. We surprised them because we arrived sooner than they expected."
Milena ballte ihre Hände zu Fäusten und stapfte weiter. Kurz darauf hielt sie erneut inne. "Clive said that Bridget was alive and well when he left her at St Mary's, right? And that he was the last one to see her alive." Sie redete in atemberaubender Geschwindigkeit weiter. "The witnesses on the *Scillonian* said that they had seen someone matching her description alive and well too."
"What do you mean?" Lauras Herz raste.
"There could have been at least half a dozen young blonde women carrying suitcases on the boat that day. Clive was the last person who definitely saw her alive. And that means . . . " Milena und Laura starrten einander an. "That means he's our **prime suspect**! He had the opportunity of killing her and of coming back to the island, saying that he had seen her get onto the *Scillonian*."
Jetzt fielen dicke Regentropfen aus düsteren Wolken, und die beiden begannen zu rennen.

---

prime suspect [praɪm 'sʌspekt] Hauptverdächtiger

"But what about his motive? Why would he kill her?", keuchte Laura.
"Maybe he wanted to own all of the island", schlug Milena schwer atmend vor.
Laura dachte darüber nach, während sie rannte. Es schien irgendwie keinen Sinn zu machen. Hätte die Polizei das nicht auch damals herausfinden müssen?
Auch Milena grübelte weiter. "But Sylvie didn't own the island until ten years later, when your father sold her everything. Nobody **commits** a murder and then waits ten years to profit from it. It doesn't make sense."
Es waren nur noch ungefähr zweihundert Meter bis zum Hotel, als Laura erschrocken stehen blieb. "Look over there. Who's that?"
Eine Frau stand nah an den Klippen. Ihr langes weißes Kleid flatterte wild im Sturm wie eine Wetterfahne.
"It's Zaphira", keuchte Milena. "What's she doing?"
Bevor sie etwas tun konnten, drehte sich die Frau um und ging mit großen Schritten zurück ins Haus. Milena und Laura rannten hinterher; es regnete immer stärker. Als sie die Tür erreichten, waren sie nass bis auf die Haut.
Die Eingangshalle war menschenleer, und plötzlich erinnerten die beiden Statuen Laura an einen Friedhof.
"Have a good night's sleep", flüsterte Milena ihr zu, als sie an ihrem Zimmer ankamen. "And make sure that you lock the door!"

---

to commit sth. [kə'mɪt] etw. begehen

Übung 25: Setzen Sie die folgenden Aussagen in die indirekte Rede.

1. Milena said, "Clive is the prime suspect."

   Milena said that Clive was the prime suspect.

2. Laura said, "Clive and Diane are lovers."

3. Sylvie said, "I don't want to know."

4. Milena said, "Life is short."

5. Laura said, "Sylvie believes her husband Clive is taking her to Australia."

6. Laura said, "Clive doesn't love Sylvie any more."

Eleven

Laura träumte in dieser Nacht vom wilden Meer mit fliegenden weißen Pferden, von Zaphira, die von den Klippen sprang, und von lauten Schreien. Schweißgebadet fuhr sie hoch, doch das Schreien hörte nicht auf. Jemand hämmerte an ihrer Tür. "Get up! Something terrible has happened."
Laura sah auf die Uhr – erst halb acht –, sprang aus dem

Bett und öffnete Milena die Tür. “What is it? What’s happened?”
Milena rannte schon wieder los, während Laura eilig in ihren Jogginganzug schlüpfte. “Just come with me. I’ll tell you on the way.”
Während sie den Gang entlangliefen, roch Laura frischen Kaffee aus der Küche. Als sie an der Rezeption angelangt waren, standen da Peter und Sylvie verschwitzt in ihrer Jogging-Kleidung. Ihre Gesichter waren kalkweiß. Sie starrten auf den Boden hinter dem Tresen. Peter flüsterte Laura zu: “It’s Mrs Rutherford. She’s dead!”
“Dead?! But how . . . ?” Ohne darüber nachzudenken, lief Laura um den Tresen herum und erstarrte. Mrs. Rutherford lag auf dem Boden. Aus einer Brustwunde war Blut auf den Marmorboden gesickert.
“She’s been shot”, flüsterte Peter. “Sylvie and I came back from jogging and found her lying here. It must have just happened. She was alive when we left.”
Laura kniete neben ihr nieder und griff nach ihrer Hand. “Get Clive, he’s a doctor!”
Peter schüttelte traurig den Kopf. “There’s no big hurry, I’m afraid. I felt her pulse. She’s definitely dead.”
Eine seltsame Ruhe breitete sich in Laura aus. Es war, als wäre ihr Kopf in Watte eingepackt. “Is there any sign of the gun?”, fragte sie ruhig.
Peter schüttelte den Kopf. “No. No sign at all.” Er hielt ein zerrissenes und blutverschmiertes Stück Stoff hoch und zeigte es ihnen. “The killer must have wrapped the gun up to **muffle** the sound and shot her **at close range**.”

---

to muffle [ˈmʌfl] dämpfen **at close range** [ət ˌkləʊz ˈreɪndʒ] aus nächster Nähe

Sylvie schluchzte. "I've known her for years. She never hurt a fly. Who could have done such a thing?"
Lauras Blick fiel auf einen Gegenstand in der Hand der Toten. "What's that? It looks like a cigarette lighter."
Sie beugte sich hinunter, um genauer nachzusehen, doch Milena bremste sie. "Don't touch the lighter. **Fingerprints**, you know!"
"We have to call the police. Oh dear. Can't somebody get Clive, please?" Sylvie schluchzte so unkontrolliert, dass Milena sie in die Arme schloss.
Peter nickte. "Okay. Where is he?"
"Still asleep, I suppose", wimmerte Sylvie. "We have separate rooms. His extension is 344."
Von der Rezeption aus wählte Peter die Nummer. Sein Blick traf sich mit dem von Laura. Auch er schien sich nicht zu wundern, als niemand abhob.
"Maybe he's out bird-watching with Wolfgang", versuchte Milena Sylvie zu beruhigen, obwohl sie, da war Laura ganz sicher, selbst nicht an ihre Worte glaubte. "Wolfgang got up very early this morning. He **slipped out** through the **French windows**. Maybe he met up with Clive somewhere."
Sylvie nickte, und in diesem Augenblick wirkte sie unglaublich verloren. Fast tonlos wisperte sie: "I thought it would be too wet to go jogging this morning, but when I got up and saw that the rain had stopped I decided to join Peter. We had just gone out of the front door when I realized that we needed fresh towels at the swimming pool. I slipped back in to leave a note for Mrs Rutherford. Just at that moment she was walking into the lobby . . . "

---

fingerprint [ˈfɪŋɡəprɪnt] Fingerabdruck **to slip out** [ˌslɪp ˈaʊt] hinausschlüpfen **French window** [ˌfrentʃ ˈwɪndəʊ] Terrassentür

Ein neuer Weinkrampf schüttelte sie, und Peter sprach an ihrer Stelle weiter. "That's right. I heard Mrs Rutherford say that she hadn't forgotten about the towels."
"What are we going to do with her?", flüsterte Milena. "We can't leave her here."
Laura sah aus dem Fenster. Es stürmte noch, und es fing gerade wieder an zu regnen. "Even if we do call the police, they won't be able to get here by boat today."
Sylvie erschrak plötzlich, starrte einen nach dem anderen an und flüsterte mit angsterfülltem Blick: "There must be a psychopath hiding somewhere on the island . . . "
Sie beendete ihren Satz nicht. Schweigend sahen sie einander an, bis Milena die Stille durchbrach: "What's that around her neck?" Sie beugte sich tiefer hinab. "I'm not going to touch it, but it looks like her zodiac pendant."
Sylvie atmete tief durch. "It's Aries, her birth sign." Sie wies wortlos auf die Vitrine mit den Sternzeichen-Souvenirs.
In dem Augenblick flog die Tür zu Diane Braggs Büro auf; sie selbst eilte heraus und starrte auf die Versammlung am Tresen. Laura sah sie entgeistert an. Konnte es wirklich sein, dass sie bis jetzt nichts von all der Aufregung mitbekommen hatte?
"What's wrong?", rief Diane panisch. "Why are you staring at me?"
Sylvie schluchzte. "Mrs Rutherford's been shot!"
Die Hysterie in Dianes Stimme steigerte sich. "Shot! How? She can't have been." Sie schien in ihr Büro zurücklaufen zu wollen, hielt dann aber inne und kam zögernd näher.
Mit einem 'Rums' öffnete sich in dem Moment die Eingangstür zur Halle, und Wolfgang und Clive stürmten prustend herein. Wolfgang war klatschnass, Clive hingegen trug

einen hellblauen Pulli und war deutlich trockener. Beide hielten inne und blickten zum Tresen. "What's up?", fragte Clive. Als er keine Antwort bekam, ging er näher heran, und Wolfgang folgte ihm. "Oh my God!", rief er, als er die Tote sah, und sein Blick irrte hilflos von Mrs. Rutherfords Körper zu Sylvie, die noch immer in Milenas Armen lag.

Clive kniete wortlos nieder, untersuchte die tote Frau und bat Diane, eine Decke zu besorgen. "We have to inform the police immediately. It is definitely a **bullet wound** . . . from a pistol, I think. It looks like . . ."

Aus einem der Gänge näherten sich Schritte, und Jean-Paul kam aus der Küche. "Has anyone here seen David?"

Clive beachtete ihn nicht. "It looks like murder."

Jean-Paul fasste sich erschrocken ans Herz und wurde bleich. "Murder? Who's talking about murder?" Er kam zum Tresen und wich wie von der Tarantel gestochen zurück, als er die Tote sah. "Alison is dead? Murdered? No, I don't believe it." Dann machte er auf dem Absatz kehrt und verschwand wieder in Richtung Küche.

"Poor Jean-Paul", wisperte Sylvie. "I can't leave him alone in this state. Maybe David can look after him. I'll ask him to make us some coffee, too."

Sie löste sich aus Milenas Umarmung und verschwand gleichfalls in Richtung Küche.

---

bullet wound ['bʊlɪt wu:nd] Schusswunde

Übung 26: Laura is thinking about the clues she has spotted. Fügen Sie die Hinweise ein.
(lighter, hear, wet, zodiac, muffle, shot, jogging)

1. Mrs Rutherford is dead. She was ______________.
2. The killer wrapped the pistol in a piece of **cloth** to ______________ the sound.
3. There is a cigarette ______________ in Mrs Rutherford's hand.
4. Sylvie and Peter went out ______________ at seven o'clock.
5. Mrs Rutherford was wearing a ______________ pendant.
6. Diane Bragg didn't ______________ anything.
7. Clive didn't get as ______________ as Wolfgang.

Einige Minuten später legte Wolfgang den Telefonhörer zurück auf die Gabel und seufzte. "As we expected, the police told me that it would be impossible to get here today. They are going to call us back in a minute to tell us what we have to do."
Während Wolfgang, Clive und Peter beratschlagten, was mit der Toten zu tun sei, sagte Laura zu Milena: "I need some fresh air, **I don't care** if it's raining."
Milena verstand. "I'll come with you."
Schon bald standen sie vor der Tür des Spa unter dem Vordach, geschützt vor dem niederprasselnden Regen.
"I've got an idea." Laura rieb sich die kalten Hände. "Let's

---

cloth [klɒθ] Stoff **I don't care.** [aɪ ˌdəʊnt ˈkeə] Es ist mir egal.

look into Diane Bragg's office through her outside window."

Sie gingen los, immer nah an der Wand des Hauses entlang; trotzdem wurden sie nass. Laura schaute zu Boden. "Look! **Footprints**!" Sie deutete auf ein sperrangelweit offen stehendes Fenster. "This must be Diane's office."

Sie schlichen weiter, obschon der Sturm ohnedies jedes Geräusch verschluckte. Es musste ein Versehen sein, dass das Fenster offen stand, denn es regnete herein. Ein ausgeklapptes Bettsofa stand in dem Büro; die Bettdecke war zerwühlt, als sei jemand schnell aufgestanden, und auf dem Bett lagen zwei Kopfkissen.

"I knew it. Clive and Diane must have spent the night together. When she came out of her office, he heard that something was going on and left through her window. Then he came in just after Wolfgang."

Milena schüttelte angewidert den Kopf. "Look at the bottle of champagne on the table and the two glasses. Were they celebrating something?"

Sie liefen zum Eingang zurück. Unter dem Schutz des Vordachs flüsterte Laura: "Do you want to know how I guessed what had happened? I've learned, through feng shui, to pay attention to little details. For instance, did you happen to notice whether Clive was wearing a light blue or a dark blue pullover when he came in?"

Milena zog nachdenklich die Stirn in Falten. "Definitely light blue. But why does that matter?"

"That's right", sagte Laura, "He was wearing a light blue **jumper**, but really, if he'd been out in the rain for any length of time, his light blue pullover should have been

---

footprint ['fʊtprɪnt] Fußabdruck **jumper** ['dʒʌmpə] Sportpullover dark blue because it would have been wet through. That meant that he'd only been out in the rain for a couple of seconds. Just long enough to climb out of Diane's window and walk in through the door."

Milena klopfte ihr auf die Schulter. "Well done, Sherlock. But what does this have to do with Mrs Rutherford's death?"

"Maybe nothing at all", erwiderte Laura achselzuckend.

"Do you think that Clive and Diane could have planned it together?"

"Who knows? But what possible motive could they have had?" Nachdenklich beobachteten sie die stürmische See und die schwarzen Wolken.

"**Has it occurred to you** that Mrs Rutherford's murder might have something to do with Bridget's disappearance? Doesn't it seem strange to you that she was found dead the day after she told you that Bridget might have been murdered?", mutmaßte Milena.

Laura erschrak, ihr fiel die ins Schloss fallende Tür ein. Hatte jemand gelauscht, als Mrs. Rutherford gestern Abend mit ihr gesprochen hatte? Vielleicht ihr Mörder. Oder die Mörderin. Oder das Mörderpaar.

"You're right. But then it must be someone who was here on the island when Bridget disappeared twenty-six years ago and is on the island today. So it would have to be Clive, Sylvie, Zaphira or Jean-Paul. So far, only Sylvie has a firm alibi. She and Peter were out jogging together."

Milena fiel noch jemand ein. "What about Helga? She knew your mother as well."

Has it occurred to you . . . ? [həz ɪt ə'kɜːd tə ˌjuː] Ist dir je in den Sinn gekommen . . . ?

Laura schüttelte nachdenklich den Kopf. "I don't think Helga or Jean-Paul are really suspects. What motive could they possibly have had? And I'm sure they don't have alibis because they were probably alone in their beds."
Plötzlich fiel ihr etwas anderes ein – etwas Schreckliches. *Wolfgang was out by himself this morning. He doesn't have an alibi for the murder either.*
Milena schüttelte gerade den Kopf. "I don't have the **slightest** idea what's going on. **Beats me!** Let's go in and see if the others have made any progress."
Entsetzt über die eigenen Gedanken folgte Laura Milena ins Haus.

Übung 27: Setzen Sie das richtige Wort ein.
(at, while, because, in, although, ago, since, for)

1. Bridget disappeared 26 years ______________.
2. Sylvie and Peter went out jogging ______________ seven o'clock.
3. Mrs Rutherford worked at the spa ______________ a long time.
4. Mrs Rutherford was murdered ______________ the morning.
5. Laura knew Clive hadn't been out in the rain very long ______________ his jumper wasn't wet through.

---

slight [slaɪt] gering **Beats me!** [ˌbiːts ˈmiː] Das ist mir zu hoch!

6. Mrs Rutherford was watching ____________ Clive and Bridget got onto the boat.

7. ____________ arriving on Rose Island, Laura has been interested in Peter.

8. ____________ Jean-Paul and Helga were on the island when Bridget disappeared, Laura doesn't suspect them.

Twelve

Als sie die Eingangshalle betraten, kam Sylvie gerade – verweint und ein Tablett mit Kaffee balancierend – aus der Küche. "David's just handed me this **tray**. He'll be joining us later. He's going to check on Jean-Paul first."
Wolfgang, Clive und Diane saßen an den Kaffeetischen. Auch Helga saß bei ihnen, war leichenblass und wirkte leicht desorientiert. Wo war Peter? Wütend schob Laura den Gedanken an ihn fort. Jetzt gab es Wichtigeres als ihre Hormonschwankungen. Eine Weile saßen sie in betretenem Schweigen beisammen und tranken ihren Kaffee. Milena verzog das Gesicht, und Sylvie entschuldigte sich. "I'm afraid the coffee's a bit on the cold side."
Milena nickte und trank ebenso wie alle anderen brav den fürchterlich dünnen, lauwarmen Kaffee.
"Have the police called back yet?", wollte Sylvie wissen.
Clive nickte. "They've just called. The Chief Inspector advised us to take photos of the body and then put it in the cold storage room. We're supposed to keep it there **under**

---

tray [treɪ] Tablett **under lock and key** [ˌʌndə ˈlɒk ən ˈkiː] hinter Schloss und Riegel

lock and key until the police arrive. Peter is just getting his digital camera now."

Laura erschrak. Mrs. Rutherford sollte in einem Kühlraum gelagert werden? Sie schauderte, schob den Gedanken entschieden beiseite und sah auf ihre Uhr. "What about Fred Lightfoot and Zaphira?"

Sylvie lachte unerwartet schrill. "Zaphira never gets up before **midday**. And Mr Lightfoot left **strict** instructions that he didn't want to be disturbed before eleven."

Milena und Laura warfen sich verstohlene Blicke zu. Die beiden hatten sicherlich auch kein Alibi für den frühen Morgen. Vermutlich hatten außer Peter und Sylvie nur Clive und Diane ein Alibi. Andererseits: Hätten sie nicht den Schuss hören müssen? Oder waren sie gerade zu sehr mit sich selbst beschäftigt gewesen? Wie dem auch sei, wenn sie sich gegenseitig deckten, würde ihre Affäre auffliegen. Oder hatten sie Mrs. Rutherford gemeinsam getötet?

Laura wandte sich an Diane. "Ms Bragg, did you happen to see Mrs Rutherford this morning before you started work? I guess you started fairly early?"

Diane sah sie irritiert an. "Yes – I mean, no. That is, I mean, I'm not sure." Sie räusperte sich und wagte nicht, Clive anzusehen. "I came down to take a swim in the morning before starting work and to be honest I didn't notice if she was at the reception desk or not. Maybe she was in her **cubby-hole**."

"Clive and I just had a look at the cubby-hole", sagte Wolfgang. "There's just a chair in it and a small table with an open magazine."

---

midday [ˌmɪd'deɪ] Mittag **strict** [strɪkt] streng **cubby-hole** ['kʌbɪhəʊl] Kabuff

"It's as if she's just **popped out** for a minute", seufzte Sylvie. Sie schien nachzudenken. "I'm really worried about Jean-Paul. This sort of thing is bad for his heart. Diane, can you go over to the kitchen and make sure David has gone to look after him?"
Diane wirkte erleichtert über die Gelegenheit wegzukommen und lief in die Küche.
Sylvie seufzte erneut. "I can't offer you much of a breakfast this morning, but I'm sure we can find some **odds and ends** in the cold storage room."
Alle schwiegen und starrten sie ungläubig an. Die Vorstellung, dass Mrs. Rutherford im selben Kühlraum wie ihr Essen lagern sollte, drehte allen den Magen um.
Sylvie gab sich einen Ruck. "Helga, I can see you're upset. Why don't you go back to bed? Clive, can you come with me? Let's try to get some work done to take our minds off what's happened. Peter can take the photos when he gets back."
Wolfgang fuhr sich durch sein noch immer feuchtes Haar. "I need to go up to my room and change. I'm getting cold." Er strich Milena über den Arm und warf im Vorbeigehen noch einen traurigen Blick auf Mrs. Rutherford; dann lief er in den Gang zu seinem Zimmer, und seine Schritte verhallten. Laura und Milena blieben allein zurück. Plötzlich stutzte Laura. "Now I know what **puzzled** me when I saw the body. Smoking isn't allowed on the island, and there were no cigarettes anywhere! So why was she holding a lighter in her hand?"
"What was that about the lighter?" Peter war mit einer Digicam zurückgekehrt.

---

to pop out [ˌpɒp ˈaʊt] kurz weggehen **odds and ends** [ˌɒdz n ˈendz] Reste **to puzzle sb.** [ˈpʌzl] jmdn. stutzig machen

"See, she's holding a lighter in her hand. But there are no cigarettes anywhere here."
"That might just mean that she was looking for a cigarette and had forgotten where she'd hidden them", überlegte Peter, während er aus verschiedenen Perspektiven Fotos von der Toten machte.
"Hidden them?"
Peter nickte. "Of course. She smoked. Ted always smuggled cigarettes in for her."
Baccy for the clerk, dachte Laura, doch dann schüttelte sie den Kopf. Wieder fiel ihr dieser Seemannsreim ein! Vermutlich war sie gerade auf dem besten Weg, den Verstand zu verlieren.
"And Sylvie would **have fired** her if she'd caught her smoking", vermutete Milena.
Peter schüttelte lachend den Kopf. "Not quite. Mrs Rutherford hid the cigarettes because otherwise Sylvie would have smoked them herself. She'**s terrified that** the guests will find out that she smokes."
Diane kam aus der Küche zurück und zu ihnen herüber. "There's something strange about this." Sie zeigte auf das Feuerzeug und dann auf den Anhänger mit dem Sternzeichen. "It might just be a weird **coincidence** but it's just occurred to me that the pendant shows Aries, the first sign of the zodiac, and Aries stands for fire – the first of the four astrological elements."
Milena sah sie fragend an. "So?"

---

to fire [ˈfaɪə] feuern **to be (was, been) terrified that** [biː / wɒz / biːn ˈterəfaɪd ðət] schreckliche Angst davor haben, dass **coincidence** [kəʊˈɪnsɪdəns] Zufall

"Well", sagte Diane, "the lighter represents fire too, doesn't it?"
"**I'm not with you.** What do you think it means?", fragte Peter.
Diane zuckte mit den Schultern. "I've got no idea. Probably nothing at all!"
Peter schüttelte den Kopf und steckte seine Kamera in die Hülle zurück. "Women", murmelte er.

Übung 28: Welche Beschreibungen gehören zusammen?

1. a lost continent	☐	**a.**	women's intuition
2. a remote island	☐	**b.**	Ruby Rose Soup
3. the prime suspect	☐	**c.**	Clive and Diane
4. a strange coincidence	☐	**d.**	Rose Island
5. an interesting relationship	☐	**e.**	Atlantis
6. a magical recipe	☐	**f.**	Clive Stone
7. a mysterious process	☐	**g.**	the pendant and the lighter

Thirteen

Als Fred Lightfoot einige Minuten später hinter Wolfgang in die Lobby rauschte, umwehte ihn ein beiger Kaftan. Er hatte tiefe Ringe unter den Augen.
"What's been going on here?", fragte er aufgeregt. "Helga just told me that I won't be getting my morning massage because Mrs Rutherford is dead. Is that true?"
Peter nickte. "I'm afraid it is true, Mr Lightfoot. And what's more, Mrs Rutherford has been killed. Murdered. See for yourself."

I'm not with you. [ˌaɪm nɒt ˈwɪð juː] Ich kann dir nicht folgen.

Er schüttelte den Kopf. "**I can't bear to look.**", sagte er angeekelt.
"I'll find David, then. He'll have to help me move the body", entschuldigte sich Peter, als Sylvie und Clive aus dem Büro kamen.
"Have you taken the photos yet, Peter?", wollte Sylvie wissen.
"You've been taking photos of that poor dead woman?" Lightfoot wurde blass. "All right. This is too much for me. How's Zaphira taking this? She's probably hysterical!"
"She's still asleep", erwiderte Sylvie nervös. "It's **just as well**. She is quite **highly strung**, you know. It would be better if the body were in cold storage before she comes down."
Freds Augen weiteten sich. "The cold storage room? Is that where you're taking her?"
Sylvie nickte, und er lief kopfschüttelnd davon.
"This will be terrible publicity for the Ruby Rose Spa", brummte Clive. "I hope I can **rely on** everyone's discretion."
Wolfgangs Stimme war eiskalt, als er ihm antwortete: "Of course you can rely on our discretion. We're not **gossips**."
Laura konnte es nicht fassen. "Are you worried about the sale price going down if the buyers find out about this, Mr Stone?"
"Clive is just as upset as anyone about Alison's death", versuchte Sylvie zu schlichten, doch niemand beachtete sie.
Peter kehrte gerade etwas verstört in die Eingangshalle zurück. "I can't find David anywhere. Maybe he's still with

---

I can't bear (bore, borne) to look. [aɪ ˌkɑːnt ˈbeə / ˈbɔː / ˈbɔːn tə ˈlʊk] Ich kann den Anblick nicht ertragen. **just as well** [ˌdʒʌst əz ˈwel] umso besser **highly strung** [ˌhaɪlɪ ˈstrʌŋ] leicht reizbar **to rely on sth.** [rɪˈlaɪ ɒn] sich verlassen auf etw. **gossip** [ˈgɒsɪp] Klatschmaul

Jean-Paul. I didn't want to knock on the door and disturb him."

Clive gab sich einen Ruck. "Well then, let me give you a hand. Let's give the poor woman some **privacy** at last."

Wolfgang bot sich ebenfalls an, beim Tragen der Leiche zu helfen, und die Frauen und Fred Lightfoot, der in einen schwarzen Anzug gekleidet zurückgekehrt war, folgten. Es sah aus wie eine Beerdigungsprozession.

In der Küche war alles sehr sauber. Die neue Kaffeemaschine stand in einer Ecke, die weiße Metalltür zum Kühlraum war verschlossen.

"Is it locked? Who's got a key?", fragte Wolfgang ächzend.

"The key's right up there! There's a stone I usually stand on to reach it", erklärte Sylvie. Dann erstarrte sie. "**Where's that stone got to**?"

Sylvie kam ohne den Stein nicht an den Schlüssel heran, der an einem Nagel oben neben der Tür hing. Für Diane hingegen war es kein Problem. Mühelos erreichte sie ihn und öffnete die Tür. Kalte Nebelschwaden schlugen ihnen entgegen.

"**Ectoplasm**!", sagte Fred andächtig.

"Ecto- what?", fragte Milena, bekam aber keine Antwort.

Die Männer trugen die Tote in den Kühlraum.

"Be careful, don't drop her", rief Sylvie. "It gets **slippery** in there sometimes."

Plötzlich rutschte Wolfgang aus; Clive und Peter konnten den Körper nicht mehr halten, und die Tote fiel mit einem dumpfen Aufprall auf die Kacheln.

"Ouch!", hörte man Wolfgang schimpfen. "There's some-

---

privacy ['prɪvəsɪ] Privatsphäre **Where has that stone got to?** [ˌweə həz ðət 'stəʊn gɒt tə] Wo ist der Stein bloß hin? **ectoplasm** ['ektəʊplæzəm] Ektoplasma **slippery** ['slɪpərɪ] rutschig

thing really hard and heavy on the floor. I've just **stubbed my toe**!"
"Oh my God!", rief Peter entsetzt. Und dann kamen die drei Männer kreidebleich aus dem Kühlraum.
"Have you just seen a ghost?", fragte Milena besorgt. "What's wrong?"
"Two ghosts, in fact", flüsterte Wolfgang.
"What do you mean?", schrie Sylvie. "What are you talking about?"
"Mrs Rutherford has got company." Selbst Clive war sehr blass. "There's already another body in there. It's David. Somebody's **smashed** his **head in** with the stone."

Außer Peter, der den Tatort und die zweite Leiche fotografierte, waren sie alle aus der Küche geflohen und versammelten sich in der Lobby. Niemand sprach. Laura wusste nicht mehr, was sie denken sollte. Sie war nur erleichtert, als Peter endlich kam.
"David was holding a pendant in his hand – a bull, a silver bull", berichtete Peter.
"Taurus", flüsterte Diane entsetzt.
"Pardon? What did you say?", fragte Peter.
"David's Taurus. I mean he *was* Taurus ... I know his birthday was in May. But he didn't believe in astrology. So why would he have that pendant ... ?" Leise fügte sie hinzu: "And the stone might represent the earth. Taurus is Earth, the second element – and the killer used a stone to kill him."
Sylvie sprang auf, ihr Stuhl kippte nach hinten und fiel mit lautem Krachen auf den Boden. "Oh my God. There's a

---

to stub one's toe [ˌstʌb wʌnz ˈtəʊ] sich die Zehe anstoßen
to smash sb.'s head in [ˌsmæʃ / ˈhed ɪn] jmdm. den Kopf einschlagen

crazy **serial killer on the loose**", kreischte sie mit angsterfülltem Blick.

Übung 29: Ordnen Sie diese Wörter den folgenden astrologischen Elementen zu. Es gibt drei Wörter pro Kategorie. *(mountain, flame, wind, lake, pool, breeze, lighter, sun, stone, sky, cliff, ice)*

1. Water ____________, ____________, ____________

2. Earth ____________, ____________, ____________

3. Fire ____________, ____________, ____________

4. Air ____________, ____________, ____________

"Now don't **exaggerate**, Sylvie!", blaffte Clive seine Frau an, und Sylvie sackte auf einem anderen Stuhl in sich zusammen. "I don't think she's exaggerating", korrigierte ihn Wolfgang. "The deaths *are* beginning to look like ritualistic serial killings."
Fred schaute Diane durchdringend an. "Does this mean that the killer is very knowledgeable about astrology?"
Nicht nur er schaute fragend zu Diane. Diese wehrte sich panisch. "Why are you all looking at me? I've got nothing to do with all of this. It's perverse. I'd be stupid to tell you all this if I were the murderer!"
Wolfgang nickte. "Calm down, everybody. Diane is right. **Basic** astrology is **common knowledge**."

---

serial killer [ˈsɪərɪəl ˌkɪlə] Serienmörder(in) **on the loose** [ɒn ðə ˈluːs] auf freiem Fuß **to exaggerate** [ɪgˈzædʒəreɪt] übertreiben **basic** [ˈbeɪsɪk] einfach **common knowledge** [ˌkɒmən ˈnɒlɪdʒ] Allgemeinwissen

Fred Lightfoot beendete das aggressive Gespräch, indem er sich erhob. Er breitete die Arme aus. "If anyone wants me, I'll be in my room meditating." Er verbeugte sich leicht und ging. Der Regen hämmerte noch immer gegen die Scheiben.

"It's like the end of the world", flüsterte Milena, und Wolfgang nahm sie beschützend in den Arm.

"Well then, who last saw David alive?", fragte er nach einer Weile des Schweigens.

"It must have been Diane", sagte Sylvie nachdenklich. "Remember? You reminded him to make sure that Jean-Paul was okay."

Diane schüttelte den Kopf. "But I couldn't find him."

"What time was that?", mischte sich Laura ein.

Sylvie überlegte. "It was just after I brought the coffee from the kitchen. And that was about half past eight. We finished the coffee and then Diane left to look for him." Sylvie schaute Diane erwartungsvoll an, die ihrem Blick standhielt.

"So it was you, Mrs Stone, who must have been the last person to see him alive. He had made the coffee, and you took it off him."

"Yes, that's right", stellte Sylvie irritiert fest. "I wondered what was taking him so long. He was just coming out of the kitchen door with the coffee when I got there. He told me that he'd had to make the coffee with the old machine because the new one **was playing up**. I took the tray off him and told him to check on Jean-Paul."

Laura wandte sich an Sylvie und Clive. "Do you think we can ask Jean-Paul if David ever came to see him?"

---

to play up [ˌpleɪ ˈʌp] verrücktspielen

Sylvie nickte. “I’ll go up to his room and see how he’s feeling. The news about David is going to hit him hard, though. Will you come with me, Clive, please?”
Clive nickte, stand auf und folgte ihr.

Schon bald kehrten sie zurück. “I’m afraid Jean-Paul has taken the news of David’s death very badly indeed. I’ve given him a light **sedative** to help him sleep”, berichtete Clive. Er wirkte ziemlich erschlagen. “Jean-Paul is very confused at the moment. We asked him about David and he isn’t sure when he last saw him.”
“Has Zaphira woken up yet?”, fragte Milena.
“What about Zaphira?” Zaphira Parsons betrat genau im richtigen Moment die Halle, natürlich mit Bouncer auf dem Arm. “What’s going on?”
Sylvie begrüßte sie so freundlich sie nur konnte. “Good morning, Zaphy. I’m afraid there have been two very sudden deaths: Mrs Rutherford and David the waiter. And what’s more, it looks as if they were both murdered.”
“Murdered? Oh my God!”
Zaphira sah aus, als wolle sie in Ohnmacht fallen. Peter lief zu ihr und führte sie zu einem Stuhl, auf den sie sich schwer fallen ließ. Er redete sehr ruhig mit ihr. “I’m afraid it’s true. The police will be here as soon as possible.”
Sylvie setzte sich neben sie. “It seems as if it’s some psychopath. A zodiac murderer. Mrs Rutherford was Aries, and David was Taurus; and . . .”
“Aaaargh!” Zaphira kreischte in einem unerträglich hohen Ton. “Then he’s going to come for me next! I’m Gemini. Oh my God!” Sie sank förmlich in sich zusammen.

---

sedative ['sedətɪv] Beruhigungsmittel

"Oh, my dear, I'd forgotten you were Gemini. Don't worry, Zaphy. Come with me – I've got some **Bach flower extracts** in my office." Liebevoll half Sylvie der aufgebrachten Zaphira auf die Beine und ging mit ihr und Bouncer in ihr Büro.
"I'm sure it's not Zaphira", murmelte Laura.
"Don't forget, she's an actress", zischte Milena.
Nach wenigen Minuten kehrte Sylvie zurück. "Zaphira's calmed down now. She's asked if she can lie down for a minute on my couch. She feels safer if she can hear people moving about in the lobby. She doesn't want to go back to her room alone." Dann horchte sie auf. "I think I heard Zaphira calling for me." Sie ging zurück. Kurz darauf hallte ein durchdringender Schmerzensschrei durch die Lobby, und Bouncer kläffte wild.
Keine fünf Sekunden später standen alle Anwesenden in Sylvies Büro. Zaphira saß heulend auf dem Sofa, Bouncer fest in den Armen. Auf dem Boden hockte Sylvie und rieb sich den Fuß.
"What happened?", rief Clive panisch.

Übung 30: Fügen Sie das richtige Wort an der richtigen Stelle ein! *(until, after, before, when)*

"**1.** ________ I came in, I tripped over Bouncer", jammerte Sylvie. "I didn't see him **2.** ________ it was too late. He was under my feet **3.** ________ I realized. **4.** ________ I fell over, I couldn't get up again. Ouch! It hurts!"

Bach flower extract [bætʃ ˈflaʊə ˌekstrækt] Bachblütenessenz

Während Clive Sylvies Fuß fachmännisch untersuchte, streichelte Zaphira ihren wimmernden Hund.
"You're lucky, it isn't broken. Probably just **sprained.** Do you think you can get up?"
Sylvie versuchte aufzustehen, knickte aber wieder um.
"I'll get you a bandage. Peter, Wolfgang, can you help her into the lobby please?" Clive warf einen Blick auf Bouncer. "And the dog? I think he's okay, isn't he?"
Zaphira drückte mit einem Seufzer Bouncer an ihre Brust.
Wolfgang und Peter brachten Sylvie in die Lobby und Clive organisierte Bandagen. Laura wollte gerade als letzte das Büro verlassen, als Zaphira plötzlich flüsterte: "Laura, there's something important I need to tell you. Can I talk to you in private this evening, please?" Sie gähnte; das Beruhigungsmittel schien zu wirken.
Laura nickte, ließ die Tür weit offen stehen und ging in die Lobby zurück, von wo aus man die Tür zu Sylvies Büro beobachten konnte. Plötzlich fiel ihr Helga ein. Sie war allein auf ihrem Zimmer. Laura zog Milena an sich heran, was niemand bemerkte, da alle sich um Sylvie geschart hatten. "I want to go and see Helga. She has some letters my mother wrote to her thirty years or so ago. Maybe I'll find something interesting in those. I want you to **stick with** Wolfgang. If there is a crazy psychopath at work here, then you could be his next **victim.**"
Milena sah sie erschrocken an. "Oh, you mean . . . ?"
Laura nickte. "Yes, because you're Gemini. If the killer is following an astrological **pattern**, then you're definitely in

---

sprained [spreɪnd] verstaucht **to stick (stuck, stuck) with sb.** ['stɪk / 'stʌk / 'stʌk wɪð] bei jmdm. bleiben **victim** ['vɪktɪm] Opfer **pattern** ['pætn] Muster

danger. Zaphira is safe down here, and I want you to be safe too!"
Milena nickte, und Laura machte sich auf den Weg. Helga öffnete sofort. Sie war immer noch im Nachthemd, und ihre Augen waren verquollen.
"I'm sorry to disturb you", entschuldigte sich Laura. "I know this must be difficult for you. You knew Mrs Rutherford quite well, didn't you? And poor David, too."
Helga schaute entsetzt. "David? What's happened to David?"
Laura erschrak. In der ganzen Aufregung war offensichtlich vergessen worden, Helga zu informieren, und nun war es an ihr, die Hiobsbotschaft zu überbringen.
Helga blieb erstaunlich gefasst. "This is awful. But don't stand there in the **corridor**, please come in."
Sie schloss sorgfältig die Tür. Ihr Reich war eine kleine Wohnung, schlicht, aber geschmackvoll eingerichtet. Helga hatte sogar eine eigene kleine Küche.
"I know it's small but it suits me. I spend all my free time in Sweden, where I've got a little house close to some woods. See, there's a picture of the house on the wall." Sie deutete auf die Fotos an der Wand. Einige zeigten ein hübsches kleines Häuschen, andere Helga mit Freunden oder Familie bei der Bescherung.
"Is that your family?"
"Yes, it is. I always spend Christmas in Sweden. My birthday is on the twenty-fourth of December, and I always go back for that."
Laura hakte nach. "Does that mean you had already left the island that December when my mother disappeared?"

---

corridor ['kɒrɪdɔː] Flur

Helga nickte. "Yes, when I left on the 19th, Bridget was still here. Bridget and Sylvie always used to give me those days off. Sylvie is an angel, too, just like your mother was. It's terrible the way Clive treats her. Flirting with that **stuck-up** Diane Bragg." Sie senkte den Blick. "Sorry, I shouldn't **speak ill of** anybody."
Laura ergriff ihre Hand. "I understand, Helga."
Helga seufzte erleichtert, dann schien ihr etwas einzufallen. "Oh, you've come for your mother's letters, haven't you? Here they are!" Sie ging zu einem Schrank und holte einen kleinen Stapel Briefe. "I think that's all. I've kept them all these years. Here you are. Take them, they belong to you now."
Laura nahm sie dankbar an. "Are you sure that you don't want me to return any of them?"
Helga schüttelte den Kopf. "I'm very sure. I've just reread them all. I hope you won't be too disappointed. The things she talks about are just little **everyday** things really."
Laura lächelte. "I'm **truly grateful** for any **memento** of my mother. My grandmother never talked about her, you see."
Helga nickte zufrieden, dann ging sie noch einmal zum Schrank und öffnete eine Schublade. Sie zog eine große Schachtel belgischer Pralinen heraus und reichte sie Laura. "Here, take this with you. I smuggle sweets onto the island occasionally. For emergencies. Chocolate **is good for the**

---

stuck-up [ˌstʌkˈʌp] hochnäsig **to speak (spoke, spoken) ill of sb.** [ˌspiːk / ˌspəʊk / ˌspəʊkən ˈɪl əv] jmdn. schlechtmachen **everyday** [ˈevrɪdeɪ] alltäglich **truly** [ˈtruːlɪ] aufrichtig **grateful** [ˈgreɪtfl] dankbar **memento** [məˈmentəʊ] Erinnerung **to be (was, been) good for the nerves** [biː / wɒz / biːn ˈgʊd fə ðə ˈnɜːvz] gut für die Nerven sein

nerves." Helga lächelte. "Your mother had a **weakness** for chocolate, too. I remember we often had little midnight **feasts** together. Otherwise she just ate organic food."

Laura lachte. "It's good to know that she wasn't perfect!"

Sie wollte gerade gehen, als Helga sie aufgeregt zurückrief. "Hold on a moment! I think your mother mentioned chocolate in the last letter she sent me! I remember finding it in my chocolate cupboard when I came back. Bridget had eaten a whole box of chocolates, if I remember correctly. She wrote me a letter **confessing** her crime."

"Is that letter among these?"

Helga blätterte hastig durch die Umschläge in Lauras Hand. "No, it isn't. I wonder where it's got to." Sie dachte angestrengt nach. "I'll try to find it. I think she mentioned doctors or something in the letter. I remember reading it and trying to **work out** what she meant . . . "

"Well, if you find it, call me. I'd really like to read it."

Helga versprach es, und obwohl Laura sie inständig bat, sich aus Sicherheitsgründen zu den anderen zu gesellen, bestand Helga darauf, in ihrer Wohnung zu bleiben. Als Laura sie verließ, hörte sie, wie Helga hinter ihr abschloss.

Übung 31: Bilden Sie Wörter aus den vorgegebenen Buchstaben.

1. Helga thinks that Bridget was an *(eganl)* ______________.

2. Helga always spends Christmas at home in *(dewsne)* ______________.

---

weakness ['wi:knəs] Schwäche **feast** [fi:st] Festessen **to confess** [kən'fes] beichten **to work out** [ˌwɜ:k 'aʊt] herausfinden

3. Bridget wrote Helga a lot of letters to help her *(piermov)* ____________ her English.

4. Helga smuggles *(wetess)* ____________ onto the island.

5. Helga is going to try to find one particular *(etretl)* ____________.

Fourteen

Laura lief eilig zu ihrem Zimmer; sie wollte allein sein, um die Briefe zu lesen. Noch immer trommelte der Regen gegen das Fenster. Sie wollte gerade zu lesen beginnen, als ihr Blick auf einen rosafarbenen Briefumschlag fiel, den jemand vermutlich unter ihrer Tür durchgeschoben hatte, während sie bei Helga gewesen war. "Laura", stand darauf geschrieben. Sie öffnete ihn. Er war von Zaphira.

Dear Laura, I have something on my **conscience**. *Twenty-six years ago, I committed a terrible crime, (Exodus 20, verse 16), and I am now paying the price. Please don't forget to come and see me this evening! Zaphira*

Ratlos starrte Laura auf die Zeilen. Sie erschrak fast zu Tode, als es klopfte. Es war Milena, die sie bereits suchte. Laura zeigte ihr den Brief, und auch Milena las ihn sorgfältig. "It sounds to me as if the brandy **has** finally **rotted** her **brain**."

"Do you think she's confessing to murder or something?"

"I'm not sure. What does Exodus 20, Verse 16 refer to?"

"I haven't the slightest idea. But maybe she saw something

---

conscience ['kɒnʃns] Gewissen **to rot** [rɒt] verrotten **brain** [breɪn] Gehirn and now she's afraid. If the killer wants to **silence** witnesses, then Zaphira is in danger. And she is a Gemini."

Milena sah sie panisch an. "Let's go and check up on her immediately. Everybody else is in the restaurant."

An Sylvies Büro angekommen, klopfte Laura leise an die jetzt geschlossene Tür.

"Nobody's answering!", wisperte sie ängstlich.

Leise öffnete sie die Tür und betrat das Büro. Auf dem Sofa lag Zaphira und schnarchte leise. Neben ihr lag Bouncer, der nur kurz sein Köpfchen hob und sich dann wieder an sein Frauchen kuschelte. Milena kicherte erleichtert. "She's alive all right!"

Am Boden vor dem Sofa stand die Thermosflasche mit dem Brandy. Laura nahm die Flasche an sich, schraubte sie auf und roch daran.

"Ugh, that's really strong stuff! We'd better leave her to sleep it off."

Sie schlichen ebenso leise davon, wie sie gekommen waren. Geistesgegenwärtig nahm Laura den Schlüssel an sich und schloss Zaphira ein. Sie wollte sie in Sicherheit wissen.

Niemand war in der Lobby. "Did you say that everyone was in the restaurant?"

Milena nickte. "All except Jean-Paul. He's still in bed, **under sedation**. Peter's checking on him now and then."

Die beiden lauschten einen Moment; leise hörten sie das Murmeln der anderen aus dem Restaurant.

"Who's your prime suspect?", flüsterte Milena.

---

to silence sb. ['saɪləns] jmdn. zum Schweigen bringen **to be (was, been) under sedation** [biː / wɒz / biːn ˌʌndə sɪ'deɪʃn] unter dem Einfluss von Beruhigungsmitteln stehen

"Still Clive, I think. If Clive killed Bridget, and if he **overheard** my conversation with Mrs Rutherford in the lobby, he would have had a motive for killing her. Maybe she or Ted the boatman saw him acting suspiciously. And he was afraid they'd tell me about their suspicions. Maybe they didn't want to mention anything to the police at the time."

Milena hielt die Luft an. "Have you ... Please **don't take this the wrong way,** but have you thought of the possibility that Clive was Bridget's secret lover?"

Laura schüttelte den Kopf. "No. I don't think that Clive would have been my mother's type. If there were anyone, I'd say it would have been Wolfgang!"

"Wolfie?", rief Milena schockiert.

Laura fasste Mut, Milena endlich mitzuteilen, was ihr schon seit einer Weile im Kopf herumging, und sie fuhr fort. "Didn't you notice the way he looked at me when I was wearing that perfume? Do you think Wolfgang could ever be **capable** of ... you know?"

Milena starrte sie ungläubig an und schüttelte den Kopf. "No, Wolfgang is a very **decent** man. There's no way he could be a murderer." Leise fügte sie hinzu: "A lover, perhaps, but not a murderer."

Die beiden lächelten einander unsicher an.

"You're right", bestätigte Laura.

"You're right, too. We were both struck by his reaction to the perfume! But let's get back to Clive as a possible mur-

---

to overhear (overheard, overheard) sth. [ˌəʊvəˈhɪə / ˌəʊvəˈhɜːd / ˌəʊvəˈhɜːd] etw. mitbekommen **Don't take this the wrong way.** [ˈdəʊnt teɪk ðɪs ðə ˌrɒŋ ˈweɪ] Versteh mich bitte nicht falsch. **capable** [ˈkeɪpəbl] fähig **decent** [ˈdiːsnt] anständig

derer. Did he have the opportunity to kill both victims?", schlug Milena vor.
Laura nickte. "Well, I'm not sure if he could have killed David. But he could have easily killed Mrs Rutherford. After all, he was sleeping in Diane's office, which is right next to the reception desk. He could have sneaked out and killed her. Maybe Diane is even in on it. And maybe she killed David! I wonder who has got a key for that little **display case** with the pendants?"
Milena stutzte. "Good question! I think Mrs Rutherford kept the key in a drawer. But the murderer could have taken the key after he'd killed her and looked up the victims' birth dates in her book."
"By the way, do you know what's happened to the pendants we found on the bodies?", fragte Laura, während sie in Richtung Restaurant gingen.
"Wolfgang made sure that they went into the hotel safe, together with the cigarette lighter!"
Als sie an der Damentoilette vorbeikamen, hielt Milena plötzlich inne. Dann zog sie Laura in den Waschraum. "Hang on, I've just got an idea, too, about this **Bible reference**, Exodus 20. I'll give my head **researcher** in New York a call. She can easily look up the reference. What's the time difference? Five hours? Then it'll be no problem." Milena tippte bereits eine Nummer in ihr Handy.
"Could you ask her to do a **background** check into all the people here, including Peter Saunders?", bat Laura.
Milena nickte, dann antwortete jemand am anderen Ende.

---

display case [dɪˈspleɪ keɪs] Schaukasten **Bible reference** [ˈbaɪbl ˌrefrəns] Bibelzitat **researcher** [rɪˈsɜːtʃə] Rechercheur(in) **background** [ˈbækgraʊnd] Hintergrund

"Oh, hi, Rosalie. It's me, Milena. Could you be an angel and do me a favour, please? **I'll be eternally in your debt** . . ."

Übung 32: Welches Wort ist das 'schwarze Schaf'? Unterstreichen Sie das nicht in die Reihe passende Wort.

1. price, praise, charge, debt
2. coast, cove, beach, thief
3. silence, peace, argument, quiet
4. notice, see, ignore, note
5. suspect, superstitious, suspicion, suspicious
6. ladder, letter, stamp, envelope

Als sie das Restaurant erreichten, sprang Wolfgang erleichtert auf. Einige der Anwesenden kauten lustlos auf ihren Pizzen herum; Sylvie zog ein schwarzes, mit Spitzen besetztes Cape enger um ihre Schultern und entschuldigte sich bei Laura und Milena. "Sorry, **folks**, I couldn't make any soup today. My **ankle** has been killing me, and I've hardly been able to walk . . . or even think."

Es war immer noch stürmisch, aber der Regen hatte nachgelassen. Plötzlich klatschte Fred Lightfoot in die Hände. "I want to go outside in a minute and do some meditation." Obwohl ihm alle abrieten, bestand er auf seinem täglichen Ritual.

"If you want to go out, Fred, you can always borrow Clive's raincoat", bot Sylvie ihm an und humpelte von ihm gestützt hinaus.

"I think I'll make myself some coffee. Anyone else for coffee?", fragte Peter, und Milena stimmte als einzige begeis-

---

I'll be eternally in your debt. [aɪl bɪ ɪ'tɜːnəlɪ ɪn jə 'det] Ich stehe auf ewig in deiner Schuld. **folks** [fəʊks] Leute **ankle** ['æŋkl] Knöchel

tert zu. Diane und Peter verschwanden mit dem dreckigen Geschirr in die Küche. Schließlich kam Peter mit zwei vollen Tassen zurück, und Milena griff dankbar danach. "Mmm, nice and hot. Just what I needed."
Laura beschlich plötzlich ein seltsames Gefühl. "Peter, where's Diane?"
"I have absolutely no idea." Er schüttelte den Kopf.
Laura und Milena sahen einander an. Diane war fort, Zaphira war fort ... Gleichzeitig sprangen sie auf, um nach Zaphira zu sehen. Als sie den Gang hinunterliefen, kamen ihnen kurz vor den Büros Sylvie und Fred entgegen; Fred in einem viel zu großen Regenmantel, Sylvie an seinem Arm hängend.
Laura hatte den Schlüssel schon in der Hand, aber Sylvie schüttelte den Kopf und breitete die Arme aus: "Don't go in there, she's asleep! What are you doing?"
"We just want to make sure Zaphira is okay", erklärte Laura und steckte den Schlüssel ins Schloss. "Maybe she wants some pizza too", fügte Milena hinzu.
"She's probably fast asleep. Why don't you wait a second while I check", schlug Sylvie ihnen vor. "She might get a shock if we all went in at once. She might think there's been another murder."
Sylvie humpelte in ihr Büro, schloss die Tür leise hinter sich und Laura, Milena und Fred vor der Nase zu. Zuerst hörten sie Bouncer jaulen, dann, wie Sylvie den Hund zu beruhigen versuchte. Und dann einen lang anhaltenden, durchdringenden Schrei.
Laura stieß die Tür auf. Sie hörte Stimmen, die anderen kamen herbeigelaufen. Vor der Couch stand Sylvie und kreischte. "I thought she was just asleep, but then I realized she wasn't breathing. She's ... dead!"

Das war unmöglich, sie hatten doch abgeschlossen! Laura begriff nichts. Zaphira lag noch genauso da, wie Laura und Milena sie zuletzt gesehen hatten.
Clive kam keuchend angerannt und schob Laura unsanft beiseite. Er beugte sich über Zaphira, um sie zu untersuchen, richtete sich dann aber schnell wieder auf. "She's been strangled ... with this **scarf**." Clive zeigte auf einen einfachen, weißen Seidenschal, der ihren Hals fest umschloss. Laura wurde kurz schwarz vor Augen, und sie stützte sich an der Wand ab, während Clive den Schal vom Hals der Toten zog und zurückwich.
"Is it another pendant?"
Clive nickte. "Gemini", flüsterte er.
Mit einem leisen "Oh ... " auf den Lippen schwankte Helga und lehnte sich an Wolfgang, der neben ihr in der Tür stand.
"Well!" Es war Diane, die gesprochen hatte. Seit wann war sie da? Wo war sie gewesen? "The murderer is being **remarkably consistent**. Zaphira is Gemini – an air sign. Air is the third element. And she was strangled. In other words – somebody cut off her **air supply**."
Laura ließ ihre Augen über die Anwesenden schweifen. Wer von ihnen könnte so etwas tun? Eine ältere Dame erschießen, einen Kellner erschlagen, eine Schlafende erdrosseln? "One thing that I'm certain of now", sagte sie schließlich, "is that all these murders have something to do with my mother's disappearance. Zaphira wanted to tell me something important this evening. But somebody knew what she wanted to do and decided to stop her." Laura fixierte jeden Anwesenden, doch niemand verhielt sich

---

scarf [skɑːf] Schal **remarkably** [rɪˈmɑːkəblɪ] bemerkenswert **consistent** [kənˈsɪstənt] konsequent **air supply** [ˈeə səˌplaɪ] Luftzufuhr auffällig – davon abgesehen, dass alle bleich waren und sie wie gebannt anstarrten.

Es war Wolfgang, der schließlich das Schweigen brach. “Let’s leave this room now. Peter, will you get your camera again, please?”

Sie wollten das Büro verlassen, da jaulte Bouncer erbärmlich auf. Sie alle hatten in ihrem Schrecken den Hund vergessen. Ohne zu zögern, nahm Peter ihn an sich. Laura lächelte ihn an, als er an ihr vorbeiging, und freute sich, dass er trotz des Horrors Verantwortungsgefühl zeigte. Einem Instinkt folgend griff Laura vor dem Hinausgehen nach Zaphiras offener Thermosflasche und roch daran. “Strange, it doesn’t smell of brandy any more. When we smelled it earlier, it smelled very strongly of brandy. Why would she bother washing out the brandy?”

Milena zuckte die Schultern. Sie sah so müde und verzagt aus, wie Laura sich fühlte. Traurig und aufgewühlt zugleich folgten sie Wolfgang in die Eingangshalle, wo Laura leise fragte: “What sign comes after Gemini, Diane?” Diane hockte müde auf einem der Bistrostühle und starrte ins Nichts. “Cancer”, murmelte sie.

“Cancer? Which one of us is a Cancer?”

“Fred, perhaps. But he was born on the cusp, so he could be Leo too.”

“When will this all stop?”, flüsterte Sylvie kraftlos. “**I can’t take it any more.** Where has Fred gone, anyway? Somebody should go out and look for him. He could be in danger.”

“I’ll go and look for him”, schlug Wolfgang vor. “Clive, Helga, Diane, will you all join me, please?”

I can’t take it any more. [aɪ ˌkɑːnt ˈteɪk ɪt enɪ ˌmɔː] Ich kann nicht mehr.

Clive nickte müde und ging, um für alle dickere Jacken zu holen.
“You two girls stay with Peter”, raunte Wolfgang ihnen zu, als er mit der kleinen Gruppe das Haus verließ. Sylvie wollte nach Jean-Paul sehen, wies Hilfe ab und humpelte mit hängendem Kopf davon.

Übung 33: Leicht verwechselbare Wörter.
Unterstreichen Sie die richtige Alternative.

1. Fred wants to *(borrow/lend)* a raincoat.
2. *(Eventually/At least)* they let him go out in the rain.
3. Peter *(cooked/made)* some coffee.
4. Fred was *(wearing/carrying)* a raincoat.
5. Laura is very *(sensitive/sensible)* to smells.
6. They don’t know who committed the *(murders/murderers).*
7. Nobody seems to be behaving *(suspiciously/superstitiously).* But that doesn’t mean that the *(murder/murderer)* is not among them.
8. Sylvie used her *(handy phone/mobile phone)* to call New York.

Kurze Zeit später saß Laura im Badeanzug am Beckenrand des Swimmingpools und las die Briefe ihrer Mutter an Helga, während Milena ihre Bahnen schwamm. Laura hatte Milena zunächst für verrückt erklärt, als sie den Vorschlag gemacht hatte, aber nun genoss sie es, hier zu sein. Peter füllte Kaffee in große Becher und reichte ihr einen davon; einen zweiten reichte er Milena, die zum Beckenrand geschwommen kam und genießerisch das Aroma einsog. Peter räusperte sich. “I really need to talk to you, because I

like you and because I trust you. I have a **confession** to make. I'm a little more than just a fitness coach."
"I knew you had something to hide", nickte Milena ruhig; Laura stutzte. Was wusste Milena, das sie nicht wusste?
"What makes you think I have anything to hide?", wunderte sich Peter.
"First of all, you're too good-looking and too clever to **bury** yourself on a remote island."
Peter grinste. "Don't be so sure. I love it here."
Doch Milena ließ sich nicht beirren. "Secondly, I just happen to know that a certain Peter Saunders is famous for writing historical books about Britain, especially Cornwall. Would that particular Peter Saunders be you, **by any chance**?" Milena tauchte unter.
Laura war unendlich erleichtert. "You're an author?"
Peter wirkte überrascht und nickte schuldbewusst. Seine Augen waren dabei so leuchtend und warm, dass Laura am liebsten sein Gesicht in ihre Hände genommen hätte.
"Well", wandte er sich dann an Milena, die inzwischen wieder aufgetaucht war, "you certainly have good **sources**! I am an author, and I'm here on a sort of working vacation. I earn a bit working as a fitness coach and a masseur – I do have qualifications for both those jobs, by the way – and I still have time to **research** the customs and traditions of the Scilly Isles. I can stay here for six months, **rent-free**, and research my book in peace. The only condition is that I include a reference to the Ruby Rose Spa in my book. That's my deal with Clive."

---

confession [kən'feʃn] Beichte **to bury** ['berɪ] begraben **by any chance** [baɪ ˌenɪ 'tʃɑːns] zufällig **source** [sɔːs] Quelle **research** [rɪ'sɜːtʃ] recherchieren **rent-free** [ˌrent'friː] mietfrei

Milena kraulte zurück und erklärte ihnen, dass sich ihre Redakteurin aus New York zurückgemeldet und Bericht erstattet hatte. Mit Schwung kletterte sie aus dem Becken, hüllte sich in einen Bademantel und fragte dann: "So, Peter Saunders, who do *you* think the murderer is?"
Er zuckte die Achseln. "Who do you think?"
Laura aber schüttelte den Kopf; sie war das Versteckspiel Leid. "To be honest, we still don't have the slightest idea who the murderer is – just a theory as to why he, or she, or even they are doing it. Mrs Rutherford and Zaphira were both going to tell me something about my mother, and they were killed. David **is the odd one out**. But maybe Mrs Rutherford or Zaphira told him something, and the murderer felt **threatened**. David might even **have caught** Mrs Rutherford's killer **red-handed**, and the murderer had no choice but to kill him too. **Whoever** it is, he or she is capable of acting quickly and **decisively**, that's for sure!"
Milena hockte sich neben sie. "By the way, my contact in New York looked up that verse from Exodus in the Bible, too. And, guess what! It's one of the Ten **Commandments**. Can you guess which one?"
"**Thou shalt not commit adultery**!", schlug Peter vor.
"Thou shalt not commit murder", versuchte es Laura.

---

to be (was, been) the odd one out [biː / wɒz / biːn ðɪ ˌɒd wʌn ˈaʊt] die Ausnahme sein **threatened** [ˈθretnd] bedroht **to catch (caught, caught) sb. red-handed** [ˌkætʃ / ˌkɔːt / ˌkɔːt / ˌredˈhændɪd] jmdn. auf frischer Tat ertappen **whoever** [huːˈevə] wer auch immer **decisively** [dɪˈsaɪsɪvlɪ] entschieden **commandment** [kəˈmɑːndmənt] Gebot **Thou shalt not commit adultery.** [ˌðaʊ ʃəlt ˈnɒt kəˌmɪt əˈdʌltərɪ] Du sollst nicht ehebrechen.

Milena schüttelte den Kopf. "Wrong! Wrong! Sorry, you'**re** both **barking up the wrong tree**. It's commandment number eight – thou shalt not **bear false witness** against thy neighbour!"
Die drei schauten sich fragend an. "That means that Zaphira **must have lied** about something. Remember that she said she saw my mother getting onto the boat? What if she was lying? What if my mother never actually left the island?"
"And what if Mrs Rutherford and Ted were lying too?", fügte Milena hinzu.

Übung 34: Fügen Sie die folgenden Wörter ein.
*(persuaded, **bribed**, owns, agreement, package, suspicious, in return, wages, expensive)*

Peter nickte. "That's possible. I swear there's something **1.** ________________ about Ted. He seems to be a bit of a smuggler in the old Cornish tradition – *watch the wall, my darling, while the gentlemen go by.*"

Laura und Milena sahen sich überrascht an. Offenbar kannte auch Peter das Schmugglerlied von Rudyard Kipling.

Peter zögerte. "I saw him giving one of the guests a small **2.** ________________. The guest gave him money in return. That's when I began to think he might be smuggling more

---

to be (was, been) barking up the wrong tree [biː / wɒz / biːn ˈbɑːkɪŋ ˌʌp ðə ˌrɒŋ ˈtriː] auf dem Holzweg sein **to bear (bore, borne) false witness** [ˌbeə / ˌbɔː / ˌbɔːn fɔːls ˈwɪtnəs] falsches Zeugnis ablegen **to lie** [laɪ] lügen **to bribe sb.** [braɪb] jmdn. bestechen than just cigarettes. He certainly **3.** ______________ an **4.** ______________ house. I don't know how he manages it on his **5.** ______________ as a boatman. But he can't have been doing this for years without anyone noticing. Maybe he had an **6.** ______________ with Clive. He could carry on smuggling drugs **7.** ______________ for saying that he saw Bridget get onto the boat. And because Mrs Rutherford was his girlfriend at the time he could have **8.** ______________ her to lie too."

Laura fiel ein, dass sie auf dem Boot beobachtet hatte, wie Ted Sylvie ein kleines Beutelchen zusteckte. Vielleicht war ja Sylvie Teds Verbündete.

Peter verfolgte seinen Gedanken weiter. "Does it mean that Clive is our man? He murdered Bridget and **9.** ______________ people to be witnesses. He might have promised Zaphira free holidays here for the rest of her life."

Laura war nicht überzeugt. "But why would Clive kill my mother?"

Milena zuckte mit den Schultern. "I don't know. I'm going to have a hot shower now, and then I'm going back to my room. I hope Wolfgang's back."

Während Milena duschte, blieb Laura mit Peter am Beckenrand sitzen. Insgeheim hoffte sie, diese Zweisamkeit mit ihm würde Ewigkeiten währen. So langsam wie nur möglich trank sie ihren Kaffee, doch das Thema, das sie beschäftigte, war weniger romantischer Natur. "We haven't found the gun Mrs Rutherford was killed with."

"Maybe the murderer threw it into the sea", vermutete Peter. "That would be sensible. We'll never find it."

Peter und Laura schauten sich an. Laura hätte ihn so gerne geküsst. Ob es ihm genauso ging? Er löste seinen Blick nicht von ihr, als er fragte: "And what about Sylvie? Do you think she's involved in all this?"

"Well, as you know, Sylvie has an alibi for the first murder – you. And she couldn't have killed Zaphira either because she was downstairs the whole time with her sprained ankle. There was always someone with her."

"But she was in the room with Zaphira alone."

"Only for a couple of seconds. Certainly not long enough to strangle her!" Laura war plötzlich müde und hungrig. Am liebsten hätte sie sich in Peters Armen zusammengerollt, um zu schlafen, doch in diesem Moment sprang Peter auf und zog sie mit sich hoch. "When Milena's had her shower, let's get into some dry clothes and pay Jean-Paul a visit. Maybe he can give us a few **pointers**."

Und für einen viel zu kurzen Moment hielt er sie in seinen Armen.

Fifteen

Peter begleitete Milena und Laura zu ihren Zimmern. Bevor Laura in ihrem verschwand, flüsterte er: "I'll help you find out what happened. I'll be back to pick you up in

---

pointer [ˈpɔɪntə] Hinweis

a few minutes. We'll go and see Jean-Paul and see what he has to say. By the way, I'd love to mention your mother in my book, if that's all right with you?"

"Of course", erwiderte sie und lächelte ihm nach. Dann schloss sie hinter sich ab.

Als sie fertig angezogen aus ihrem Badezimmer kam, hörte sie Stimmen im Gang. Vermutlich waren die anderen zurückgekehrt.

Aber es klang wie ein verhaltenes Streitgespräch. Zwei Frauen gingen offensichtlich gerade an ihrem Zimmer vorbei. Laura wagte nicht, die Tür zu öffnen, erkannte aber die aufgeregte Stimme von Helga. "I've just found this letter from Bridget. At the time I didn't understand the meaning of the word 'doctor', but now I do."

Helga hatte also den letzten Brief ihrer Mutter gefunden. Aber wem erzählte sie das gerade? Laura riss, ohne zu zögern, ihre Zimmertür auf; Helga und Sylvie starrten sie an wie einen Geist. Dann drehte Sylvie sich um und ging langsam hinkend den Gang hinunter. "The storm seems to **have died down** so I'm sure the police will arrive some time today. Come on, Helga, I need your help in the kitchen."

Helga wollte Sylvie folgen, den Brief in der Hand, Laura ging in die Offensive. "Is that the letter from my mother? You know, the one you couldn't find?"

Aber Helga sah an ihr vorbei und stammelte. "No, no. It's a different letter." Dann eilte sie hinter Sylvie her.

Nachdenklich ging Laura zurück in ihr Zimmer und verschloss sorgfältig die Tür. Warum hatte Helga gelogen?

---

to die down [ˌdaɪ ˈdaʊn] sich legen

Peter kam wenige Augenblicke später, und gemeinsam gingen sie zu Jean-Paul, betraten auf sein Brummen hin das Appartement und blieben überrascht an der Tür stehen. Jean-Paul lag nicht wie erwartet in seinem Bett, sondern saß in einem Sessel. Überall verstreut lagen Fotos und Zeitungsausschnitte, die er gerade zu sortieren schien.
"Come closer, Laura, my dear, and have a look. These are all **press cuttings** about the spa. The first one goes back almost thirty years. I've always meant to put them in an album." Jean-Paul hielt einen Artikel mit einem Foto von einer blonden Frau hoch.
"Is that my mother?" fragte Laura irritiert.
Jean-Paul schüttelte den Kopf. "No, that's Sylvie in her biggest role. Look at the headline underneath: 'Mademoiselle Lafleur Turns **Hotelier**'!"
Laura reichte den Artikel mit einem vielsagenden Blick an Peter weiter. "Sylvie certainly looks blonde there, doesn't she!"
"It's a **wig**", erklärte Jean-Paul ihnen und fuhr fort: "I met her in France just before she got the part of Mademoiselle Lafleur. She had no trouble playing a French woman because she'd lived in France for so long."
Bewunderung schwang in seiner Stimme mit, und Laura stockte der Atem. "Oh – so she isn't originally French then?"
"No, she's from Scotland originally, but she lost her accent very quickly. She's very good at imitating accents, too. You should hear her do Kylie Minogue!"
Laura hockte sich neben ihn auf die Sessellehne. "Jean-

---

press cutting ['pres ˌkʌtɪŋ] Zeitungsausschnitt **hotelier** [həʊ'telɪeɪ] Hotelbesitzerin **wig** [wɪg] Perücke

Paul, I was just wondering if you have any memories of Bridget."
Er ließ die Zettel sinken und schaute Laura an. "Bridget was a very determined person. She loved her natural ingredients and organically grown **produce**. In those days it wasn't as trendy as it is now. She was ahead of her time." Er hielt inne. "I'm sorry but I really can't remember the last time I saw her. The day she vanished we were having a bit of a crisis in the kitchen. Sylvie **came down with** food poisoning. She didn't get up all day. I don't know what caused it. She and Zaphira were the only ones to get it. I felt terrible. I went to her bedroom a couple of times and knocked, but there was no answer. She must have been really ill." Wieder machte er eine Pause, bevor er leise fortfuhr. "Things were probably too hectic for Bridget to say a proper goodbye to me and I was too busy trying to find out the reason for the food poisoning."
Laura stand auf. Sie konnte sich nicht vorstellen, dass ihre Mutter sich damals nicht von Jean-Paul verabschiedet hätte – wenn es ihr möglich gewesen wäre ... Er sah sie mit seinen treuen Augen an, und in diesem Augenblick tat ihr der alte Koch unendlich leid. Sie drückte ihm einen Kuss auf die Stirn. "Thank you, Jean-Paul. Thanks a lot."
Ein Lächeln huschte über Jean-Pauls Gesicht.
Laura war erstaunt über sich selbst; so etwas hatte sie noch nie in ihrem Leben getan. "I've just got one more question. Do you drink coffee in the morning? Or did David?"
Jean-Paul schüttelte den Kopf, sichtlich irritiert über die

---

produce ['prɒdju:s] (Natur-)Erzeugnis **to come (came, come) down with sth.** [ˌkʌm / ˌkeɪm / ˌkʌm 'daʊn wɪð] an etw. erkranken

seltsame Frage. "We both preferred tea in the morning, just like Alison Rutherford."
Laura nickte, als ob sie damit gerechnet hätte. "You've been a huge help, thanks again."
Er schaute sie überrascht an. "I have? Well, it was a pleasure."
Peter, der immer noch unauffällig an der Tür wartete, räusperte sich. "Oh and by the way, do you remember now when you last saw David?"
Jean-Paul schüttelte seinen Kopf. "I**'ve been racking** my **brains** about it, but I think the sedative has affected my memory. I can't remember if he really came into my room, or whether I just dreamed it!"

Übung 35: Gesucht wird . . .
Beantworten Sie folgende Fragen zum Text.

1. Who's been racking his brains trying to remember something?

____

2. Who's very good at imitating accents?

____

3. Who owns a blonde wig?

____

4. Who came down with food poisoning the day Bridget disappeared?

____

---

to rack one's brains [ˌræk wʌnz ˈbreɪnz] sich den Kopf zerbrechen

5. Who wants to mention Bridget in his book?

____

6. Who might have caught Mrs Rutherford's killer red-handed?

____

Laura und Peter verließen den Raum, und Laura zog aufgeregt die Tür hinter sich ins Schloss. Verwundert sah Peter sie an. "What's up, Laura?"
"There were several witnesses who saw Clive leaving the island with a blonde woman who, from the distance, everyone assumed was my mother", sprudelte es aus ihr heraus. "Now I'm sure it was Sylvie! Jean-Paul said she was in bed all day. Nobody saw her. And she was the one most likely to own a blonde wig."
Peters Augen weiteten sich. "But what does all that mean?"
Laura schaute sich um und lauschte einen Augenblick. Alles war ruhig. Dann flüsterte sie weiter. Sie wusste gar nicht, wo sie anfangen sollte, aber sie musste all die neuen Informationen sortieren. "My mother **valued** pure, organic ingredients, right? That made me think of the conversation I overheard between Sylvie and Helga. Helga said that at first she hadn't understood the meaning of the word 'doctor'. In that missing letter I told you about, remember? I thought that was strange because even if your English is bad you would normally know that word. It's pretty international ... well, you can interpret the word differently too. I'm doing some work for a Canadian businessman and

---

to value ['vælju:] schätzen

I remember once, when he offered me some coffee, he said, 'Be careful, I'**ve doctored** it!'"

Jetzt begann auch Peter die Zusammenhänge zu begreifen. "To doctor something means to add some ingredient that doesn't normally belong there. Right?"

"Right", bestätigte Laura. "He'**d poured** in some whiskey! Maybe my mother mentioned in that letter that Clive was doctoring the food!"

"Maybe he was adding some kind of **appetite suppressant** to the soup", vermutete Peter. "And maybe, when Bridget found out, he killed her. Sylvie loved him so much that she decided to help him."

Lauras Herz drohte für einen Moment auszusetzen, als sie jetzt an Helga dachte. Sie lief los und zog Peter hinter sich her. "Come on! We're such idiots. We have to find Helga before Sylvie tells Clive that she has the letter. Helga could be in real danger."

Gefolgt von Peter rannte sie zum Zimmer von Wolfgang und Milena. Sie hämmerte gegen die Tür. "Please come to the lobby", rief sie, und dann eilte sie mit Peter weiter in die Eingangshalle, und sie schauten sich um. Es war niemand zu sehen, aber auf dem Tresen lag ein Blatt Papier. Peter griff danach und las. "What do you make of this – *Helga Svensson, born in Gallarp, Sweden, 24/6/1950.* It looks like Helga's **employment record**." Peter wedelte nervös mit dem Zettel. "I don't like this. Why would Clive print out her employment record now? Does she want to leave?"

---

to doctor ['dɒktə] herumdoktorn an **to pour** [pɔː] gießen **appetite suppressant** ['æpɪtaɪt səˌpresnt] Appetitzügler **employment record** [ɪm'plɔɪmənt ˌrekɔːd] Dienstakte

Laura wurde fast übel vor Angst. "What was the date of birth on the employment record?"
"June 24", antwortete Peter. "Oh my God, that makes her Cancer – Aries, Taurus, Gemini, Cancer. The zodiac murderer could **strike** again!"
In diesem Moment kamen Wolfgang und Milena in die Halle gerannt.
"We have to find Clive", rief Laura ihnen entgegen, als plötzlich die Tür zu Dianes Büro aufflog und Clive und Diane in der Tür standen.
Wie bestellt kam aus einem anderen Gang Fred Lightfoot angelaufen. "What's going on? Is dinner ready yet?" Völlig durcheinander blickte er von einem zum anderen, aber niemand nahm Notiz von ihm.
Peter ging auf Clive zu und packte ihn am Hemd. "Dr Stone, what have you done with Helga? Where is she? Did you murder her, too?"
"Murder? Are you accusing me of murder? That's **ridiculous**!" Dr. Stone wurde blass. Diane ergriff seine Hand und hielt sie fest. Peter lockerte den Griff.
"You murdered Bridget because she caught you doctoring the soup. It would have been totally **unacceptable** to her to have her pure organic meals **adulterated**."
Diane drängte sich zwischen Peter und Clive. "Stop – this is **madness**. Clive has never killed anybody in his life. How can you say such a thing?"
"You're in it together, aren't you?", mischte sich Milena ein. "What about those pendants?"

---

to strike (struck, struck) [straɪk / strʌk / strʌk] zuschlagen **ridiculous** [rɪˈdɪkjʊləs] lächerlich **unacceptable** [ˌʌnəkˈseptəbl] untragbar **to adulterate** [əˈdʌltəreɪt] *hier:* verfälschen **madness** [ˈmædnəs] Wahnsinn

Diane schüttelte panisch den Kopf: "But you can easily get them from reception. Anyone could **gain access** to the key of the display case if they were really determined. And I would have to be pretty stupid to explain the **significance** of the pendants, wouldn't I?" Sie klammerte sich an Clive. "And anyway, neither Clive nor I could have killed Mrs Rutherford. As you've probably guessed, we love each other. The morning Mrs Rutherford was murdered we were in bed together."

"Well, that's hardly a **cast-iron** alibi, is it?", bemerkte Peter trocken.

Clives Gesicht wurde rot vor Wut. "Neither Diane nor I have murdered anybody. Why, for God's sake? Sylvie and I are selling the spa at the end of the year, and these murders **will** just **drive** the price **down**! I have absolutely no motive to do such a **harebrained** thing! **On the contrary**!"

Wolfgang sah ihn kalt an. "And you have nothing to hide as far as Bridget's disappearance is concerned?"

Clive starrte zurück. "No. Absolutely not. Laura, you just have to accept that Bridget had a lover. Maybe it was even your dear 'Uncle' Wolfgang?"

Laura wurde immer nervöser. So viel kostbare Zeit verging. Wo war Helga?

Peter ließ nicht locker. "Dr Stone, do you **deny** that the woman you took to St Mary's twenty-six years ago wasn't Bridget, but was, in fact, Sylvie? Sylvie wearing a blonde wig?"

---

to gain access to sth. [geɪn 'ækses] sich Zugang verschaffen zu etw. **significance** [sɪg'nɪfɪkəns] Bedeutung **cast-iron** [ˌkɑːst'aɪən] *hier:* sicher **to drive (drove, driven) down** [draɪv / drəʊv / 'drɪvn] drücken **harebrained** ['heəbreɪnd] verrückt **on the contrary** [ɒn ðə 'kɒntrərɪ] im Gegenteil **to deny** [dɪ'naɪ] bestreiten

Clive sah ihn fassungslos an. "How did you . . . ?"
Laura konnte sich nicht mehr bremsen. "Where is Helga?", schrie sie, und Peter fuchtelte mit dem Zettel vor Clives Nase herum.
"Why did you print out Helga's employment record? Where is she?"
Clives Blick wanderte unstet zwischen Laura und Peter hin und her. "Helga's employment record? What do you mean? I never printed anything out. I've been with Diane the whole time. I don't know where Helga is!"
Laura warf erneut einen Blick auf das Blatt und starrte auf das Geburtstagsdatum. Und plötzlich wusste sie, dass er nicht log. Ihr Herz raste.
"So that's it! Now I understand everything – the smell of coffee and brandy. It's like a **jigsaw puzzle**. But there's still one piece missing. I have to be sure . . . ", flüsterte sie entsetzt. "Peter, can you tell me exactly what Mrs Rutherford said just before you and Sylvie went jogging?"
Alle starrten sie an, als ob sie verrückt geworden sei.
Peter versuchte offenbar, einen klaren Gedanken zu fassen. "Let me see . . . Sylvie asked her to organize fresh towels, and I heard Mrs Rutherford say: 'Don't worry, Mrs Stone. I haven't forgotten the towels.' That's all I remember."
"Hurry!", murmelte Laura jetzt und stolperte in Richtung Küche. Dorthin hatte Helga gehen wollen.
Mit Sylvie. "There's no time to lose!"
Und dann rannte sie vorwärts, als ginge es um ihr Leben.

---

jigsaw puzzle ['dʒɪgsɔː ˌpʌzl] Puzzle(spiel)

Übung 36: Laura is about to solve the case!
Welche der folgenden Hinweise haben ihr geholfen (✓)? Und welche sind falsche Fährten (×)?
Wenn Sie alle Hinweise beisammen haben, können Sie den Fall auch lösen.

1. ☐ The statues in the hall
2. ☐ Sylvie's wig
3. ☐ The smell of coffee in the lobby
4. ☐ The name of the boat
5. ☐ The bottle of brandy
6. ☐ The employment record
7. ☐ The Cornish doll

Sixteen

Als sie alle in die Küche stürmten, stand Sylvie summend an der Kaffeemaschine. Laura verlor keine Zeit mit Höflichkeiten. "Where's Helga, Sylvie? And where's the letter?"
Sylvie drehte sich überrascht um, lächelte und zog ihr schwarzes, spitzenbesetztes Cape enger um die Schultern.
Laces for a lady, letters for a spy!
"I have no idea where Helga is and I don't know what letter you mean, my dear Rhiannon!"
Dann fiel ihr Blick auf Clive und Diane, die einander an den Händen hielten, und ihr Gesicht verfinsterte sich. Sie drehte sich abrupt um und fummelte nervös an der neuen Kaffeemaschine herum.
"You're good at making coffee, aren't you, Sylvie? After all, you made a whole pot of it just after Mrs Rutherford was murdered."
Als Sylvie ihr widersprechen wollte, winkte Laura ab. "You

pretended that it was David who made it. I could smell coffee when I came down to the reception. And neither Jean-Paul nor David drink coffee in the morning."
Sylvie musterte sie mit einem arroganten Gesichtsausdruck und fuhr fort, an den Knöpfen der Maschine herumzunesteln. "I don't understand what you're talking about. I'm just going to make everybody some coffee now."
Laura schrie sie an. "Where's Helga? What have you done with her? Have you killed her, too – like you killed the other zodiac victims?"
Sylvie berührte, aus Versehen wie es schien, einen heißen Teil der Maschine und schrie laut auf, dann streckte sie die sich langsam rötende Hand vorwurfsvoll Laura entgegen. "Look what you've done! I've burned my hand – it's going all red!"
Doch Laura verspürte keinerlei Mitleid. "It looks like blood on your hands, Sylvie! Mrs Rutherford's blood! David's blood! Zaphira's blood! And, if I'm right, my mother's blood, too. What have you done with Helga?"
Sylvies Blick wanderte von Laura zu den anderen. Niemand sprach.
"Little Rhiannon's gone mad. I've never killed anybody", lächelte sie.
"You were the last person to be seen with Helga. She's disappeared. Where is she?", mischte sich jetzt Peter ein.
Tödliches Schweigen legte sich über den Raum. Sylvie starrte Laura hasserfüllt an. "Who do you think you are, Laura? You have no right to stand there making ridiculous **accusations**. You have no right to even be here. Your fa-

---

to pretend [prɪ'tend] vorgeben **accusation** [ˌækjʊ'zeɪʃn] Anschuldigung ther – **drunkard** that he was – sold me his part of the hotel. He practically **begged** me to take the island off his hands as well." Sie lachte, und es klang kalt und böse. "All he needed was a bottle of whiskey, and he would have signed his **soul** away. What am I saying? A bottle – ha! – **a wee dram** was all he needed – and he was ready to sign both **contracts**." Sylvie stampfte auf wie ein kleines Kind. "Get out of my kitchen. I didn't kill Bridget, and even if I had, you can't prove anything. Her body was never found. And as for the zodiac murders", sie zeigte mit dem Finger auf Diane, "it was her, of course. She's crazy. She wants to ruin my **reputation** and the reputation of the Ruby Rose Spa. She's **jealous** of me and my success, so she's killing my **staff** and my friends off in astrological **sequence**. She wants to ruin me and run off with my husband."

"Stop, Sylvie!" Clive machte einen vorsichtigen Schritt auf sie zu. "Diane and I love each other. I've tried to tell you but you never listened."

Sylvie lächelte verstört und näherte sich ihm. Ein Wimmern entrang sich ihrer Kehle und wurde binnen Sekunden zu einem lauten Kreischen. Wie eine Furie schlug sie auf ihn ein. "Love? Has love made you blind, Clive? Diane is a **murderess**. Remember the pendants? She's the one who bought them in the first place. She's jealous of me – of us. She wants to **split** us **up**. Open up your eyes . . . "

---

drunkard ['drʌŋkəd] Säufer **to beg** [beg] betteln **soul** [səʊl] Seele **a wee dram** [ə 'wi: ˌdræm] ein kleiner Schluck **contract** ['kɒntrækt] Vertrag **reputation** [ˌrepjʊ'teɪʃn] Ruf **jealous** ['dʒeləs] eifersüchtig **staff** [stɑ:f] Personal **sequence** ['si:kwəns] Reihenfolge **murderess** ['mɜ:dərəs] Mörderin **to split (split, split) up a couple** [ˌsplɪt / ˌsplɪt / ˌsplɪt 'ʌp ə ˌkʌpl] ein Paar auseinander bringen

Clive griff nach Sylvies Armen und hielt sie fest. “It’s over, Sylvie. Diane and I are definitely leaving together. I’m sorry. And, by the way, I know Diane isn’t the murderer. The morning Mrs Rutherford was killed, we were together – together all night, on the sofabed in her office. Diane couldn’t have killed Mrs Rutherford. Her alibi is as good as yours.”
Sylvie starrte ihren Mann verzweifelt an und klammerte sich an ihn. Lauras Herz klopfte wie verrückt. Wo war Helga?
“I hate to correct you, Dr Stone, but in fact Sylvie has no alibis for any of the murders.”
Alle starrten Laura ungläubig an, selbst Milena. Dann schrie Laura. “Where is Helga?” Sie schrie, so laut sie nur konnte. Danach fiel tödliches Schweigen über die ganze Gruppe.
Sylvie ließ ihren Mann los und wollte auf Laura zugehen; und dann hörten sie es. Alle hörten es. Da war etwas, wie ein leises Klopfen. Sylvie wurde kreidebleich.
“Over there”, rief Peter und rannte zum Kühlraum. “There’s somebody locked in the cold storage room!”
Er griff nach dem Schlüssel und riss die Tür auf. Helga fiel ihm entgegen, mit weit aufgerissenen Augen, zitternd und bleich wie der Tod. “Chrgh”, krächzte sie, dann fiel sie ohnmächtig in Peters Arme. Er trug sie in den Raum und bettete sie sanft auf den Boden.
“Everything will be okay”, murmelte er und strich ihr über die kalte Stirn.
“Is she . . . ”, fragte Milena mit Panik in der Stimme.
“No, she isn’t”, antwortete Clive, der sich jetzt ebenfalls über Helga gebeugt hatte.
“Look”, rief Diane entsetzt, “There’s a pendant around her neck. Cancer.”
“Peter”, befahl Clive, “go and get some blankets quickly. Wolfgang, please, we need hot water.”

Bevor Peter die Küche verließ, flüsterte Laura ihm etwas zu. Er schaute irritiert, nickte dann aber. "I'll get it!"

Übung 37: Sind die folgenden Aussagen wahr (✓) oder falsch (×)?

1. ☐ Sylvie burned her foot.
2. ☐ Sylvie has a lace cape.
3. ☐ Sylvie thinks that Diane is jealous of her.
4. ☐ Helga is found dead.
5. ☐ Helga is wearing a zodiac pendant.
6. ☐ Laura says something to Peter quietly.

Sylvie kreischte: "Diane – this is all your fault. You killed Mrs Rutherford when Clive was asleep."
Doch Diane schüttelte nur stumm den Kopf.
Laura versuchte Ruhe zu bewahren, ihr fehlte nur noch eine letzte Information. "Clive, can you tell me who has access to the **personnel records**?"
Clive, der mittlerweile seine Jacke ausgezogen und über Helga gelegt hatte, antwortete beiläufig: "Only Sylvie and I. Those records are kept strictly confidential."
Peter kam zurück mit Decken und einem eingerahmten Foto, das er Laura überreichte. Laura hielt es hoch, sodass alle es sehen konnten. "This is a photograph taken from Helga's room. As you can see, the photo was taken at Christmas time, and Helga is sitting with her family around the Christmas tree, opening presents."
Fred Lightfoot starrte auf das Foto. "What's unusual about that? Everyone opens Christmas presents at Christmas."
Laura nickte. "That's true. But in this case it's not a Christ-

---

personnel record [ˌpɜːsəˈnel ˌrekɔːd] Personalakte

mas present. It's a birthday present! Helga's birthday is on the 24th of December. Now, I don't know much about astrology, but we have an expert in our midst. Diane, would you say that somebody born on the 24th of December is likely to be Cancer?"
Diane schüttelte den Kopf. "No way. Helga is a Capricorn."
"Only two people could have changed the date of birth on Helga's records." Mit diesen Worten zog Laura den Zettel, den Peter auf dem Tresen in der Eingangshalle gefunden hatte, hervor und fuhr fort. "**Namely**, Clive or Sylvie. Only these two people had access to them. And whoever changed the records also pushed Helga into the cold storage room, knocked her unconscious and put the pendant round her neck. Luckily she **regained consciousness** long enough to **tap** on the door."
Clive war aufgesprungen und starrte auf Sylvie. "You! I never would have believed it! You! A murderer! Did you kill Bridget, too? You always said it was an accident."
Sylvie wimmerte und jaulte wie ein getretener Hund. Es klang schauerlich.
"It *was* an accident, Clive. She knew you were adulterating the soup. She gave me an ultimatum – either you **pulled out** of the spa completely, or she would tell the police. It was the 20th of December. I asked her to meet me that evening on the cliff path next to the cairn. She agreed." Sylvie heulte und wimmerte.
Lauras Herz klopfte. Nun würde sie endlich erfahren, was mit ihrer Mutter damals geschehen war. Ihre Augen suchten

---

namely [ˈneɪmlɪ] nämlich **to regain consciousness** [rɪˌgeɪn ˈkɒnʃəsnəs] wieder zu sich kommen **to tap** [tæp] leicht klopfen **to pull out** [ˌpʊl ˈaʊt] aussteigen

Peter; er schob sich wie gerufen an ihre Seite und nahm sie ungefragt in den Arm. Sie fühlte sich bei ihm so sicher wie nie zuvor in ihrem Leben. *Vielleicht so sicher wie die kleine Rhiannon in den Armen ihrer Mutter*, dachte sie, doch dann wimmerte Sylvie weiter. "Bridget came up the cliff path, and I was waiting next to the cairn. We argued. She said she was determined to **get rid of** you, Clive. She couldn't trust you any more. I **pleaded** with her to give you a second chance."
Alle schauten zu Clive. "It's in the salt", flüsterte er beschämt. "I just wanted to make sure the spa was a success. We had both **invested** so much money in it. I couldn't just rely on some weird 300-year-old herbal recipe. So I added an appetite suppressant. Not a dangerous **dose**. Just enough to do the job."
Sylvie nickte. "I tried to explain that to Bridget, but as far as she was concerned, you were committing some horrible crime. She was getting really upset and I couldn't calm her down. Suddenly she stumbled and I realized that she was standing on the edge of the cliff. Really, I tried to hold on to her. But she lost her balance. She went **tumbling down** into the dark sea. It all happened so quickly that I didn't have time to think."
Clive starrte auf den Boden. "Sylvie came in, wet and screaming, and told me everything. Eventually we came up with a plan. Bridget was supposed to leave for Hamburg the next day. It was easy to pretend that Sylvie was in her room suffering from a bad case of food poisoning. We made Zaphira pretend that she was ill, too. To make it

---

to get (got, got) rid of sb. [ˌget / gɒt / gɒt ˈrɪd əv] jmdn. loswerden **to plead** [pliːd] flehen **dose** [dəʊs] Dosis **to tumble down** [ˌtʌmbl ˈdaʊn] hinabstürzen sound **convincing**. Sylvie still had her blonde wig from the time she played Mademoiselle Lafleur. She put it on and pretended to be Bridget. We took the boat to St Mary's. Sylvie even went aboard the *Scillonian*, so that people would notice a blonde woman carrying a suitcase."

Sylvie flüsterte. "And then I went to the **Ladies'**. I had **a change of clothes** in the suitcase and I took off the wig. Then Clive and I came back to Rose Island. It was dark already. I sneaked up the steps and slipped back into my room. **We had everybody fooled**. Especially the police." Sie schaute Laura entschuldigend an. "After all, Bridget was dead. And it was an accident. But who would believe us. We had to protect ourselves. I didn't think we were doing anybody any **harm**."

Eine abgrundtiefe Enttäuschung überflutete Laura. "No harm!", flüsterte sie. "If only you knew, Sylvie. If only you could feel my pain, my grandmother's pain, my father's pain. You ruined our lives. My father couldn't bear to go on living, not knowing what had happened to my mother ... **His life became a living hell**."

Es war mucksmäuschenstill in der Küche, und alle sahen zu Laura. Sogar Sylvie hatte aufgehört zu wimmern und lauschte ihr. Ruhig sprach Laura weiter. "So, the guests **were convinced** it was my mother who had left with Clive.

---

convincing [kən'vɪnsɪŋ] überzeugend **Ladies'** ['leɪdɪz] Damentoilette **a change of clothes** [ə ˌtʃeɪndʒ əv 'kləʊðz] Kleiderwechsel **We had everybody fooled.** [wɪ həd ˌevrɪbɒdɪ 'fuːld] Wir haben alle an der Nase herumgeführt. **harm** [hɑːm] Schaden **His life became a living hell.** [hɪz 'laɪf bɪˌkeɪm ə ˌɪvɪŋ 'hel] Sein Leben wurde zur Hölle. **to be (was, been) convinced** [biː / wɒz / biːn kən'vɪnst] überzeugt sein

You got your friend Zaphira to give a statement to the police that she had seen Bridget up close."
Clive nickte. "Zaphira was always short of money. That and the promise of free holidays once a year was enough." Er zögerte, bevor er fortfuhr. "I gave Ted the day off, and he was happy because he could fool around with his girlfriend. I didn't realize that they were watching us from the cliffs. At first I was glad of the two extra witnesses – but then he started to **blackmail** me. He said that the blonde woman who got on the ferry walked in a different way to Bridget."
Clive ballte seine Fäuste. "Ted's an **observant** little **sod**."
Sylvie sah Laura traurig an. "I was afraid of being accused of murder. It was an accident, I swear. But I wouldn't **have survived** the **separation** from Clive if they'd sent me to prison." Clive wagte es nicht, ihren Blick zu erwidern.
"I believe you, Sylvie", flüsterte Laura. "I do so want to believe that my mother's death was an accident. But what about the other three?"
Wie auf Knopfdruck kreischte Sylvie wieder. "I didn't do anything! Really, I didn't do anything! You can't prove that I did – I've got alibis!" Sie klang auf einmal trotzig.
Laura sah sie lange an. "I'm very sorry, Sylvie, but I can prove it." Sie drehte sich um und ging in Richtung Lobby; die anderen folgten ihr schweigend. Wolfgang und Fred schleiften Sylvie mit, die sich nach Kräften wehrte, während Clive und Peter die noch immer bewusstlose und in Decken gehüllte Helga auf das Sofa im Büro betteten. Na-

---

to blackmail sb. ['blækmeɪl] jmdn. erpressen **observant** [əb'zɜːvnt] aufmerksam **sod** [sɒd] Dreckskerl **to survive** [sə'vaɪv] überleben **separation** [ˌsepə'reɪʃn] Trennung

türlich hatte Sylvie auf einmal keinerlei Schmerzen mehr in ihrem Fußgelenk, und es überraschte niemanden.
Als sie alle in der Lobby versammelt waren, sagte Clive: "I've phoned the police. They'll be arriving in about half an hour."

Übung 38: Bringen Sie die Ereignisse der Handlung in die richtige Reihenfolge.

1. ☐ Bridget and Sylvie had a serious argument.
2. ☐ Sylvie sneaked back to Rose Island with Clive.
3. ☐ Sylvie arranged to meet Bridget near the cairn.
4. ☐ Bridget found out that Clive was adulterating the soup.
5. ☐ Bridget gave Sylvie an ultimatum.
6. ☐ Ted started to blackmail Sylvie and Clive.
7. ☐ Sylvie put on a blonde wig and left the island with Clive.
8. ☐ Bridget stumbled and fell off the cliff to her death.

Alle setzten sich an die Tische zwischen die Palmen. Für den Bruchteil einer Sekunde erinnerte sich Laura an ihre Ankunft hier. Es waren in Wahrheit nur wenige Stunden vergangen, aber sie fühlte sich, als seien es Jahre gewesen.
Dann begann sie, den anderen die Fakten darzulegen, die sie zusammengetragen hatte. "When I arrived here, Mrs Rutherford soon realized that I was Bridget's daughter. **Impulsively**, she decided to let me know about Ted's suspicion that my mother was murdered. Sylvie **was eavesdrop-**

---

impulsively [ɪm'pʌlsɪvlɪ] spontan **to eavesdrop** ['i:vzdrɒp] lauschen

ping on our conversation. That was when Sylvie realized she had to stop her."
"But Peter gives me the perfect alibi", wimmerte Sylvie. "He saw Mrs Rutherford alive in the lobby and we were jogging together the whole time until we returned and found her dead!"
Laura sah zu Peter hinüber. "You said that you *heard* Mrs Rutherford talking before you went jogging with Sylvie. But did you actually *see* her?"
"Well, no, come to think of it, I didn't see her at all. I only heard her voice. But it was **unmistakably** Mrs Rutherford. Very **high-pitched**."
Peter sah sie verzweifelt an, er befürchtete offensichtlich, ihr mit seiner Aussage keinen Gefallen getan zu haben.
"**Let me get this straight**", sagte sie. "You saw Sylvie pop her head around the door, and you heard her say something. Then you *heard* Mrs Rutherford answer."
Als Peter nickte, fuhr Laura fort, "We all know that Sylvie used to be an actress. And she's extremely good at imitating voices. Jean-Paul told us how she **entertains** people by **impersonating** celebrities."
Laura hielt inne. Man hätte eine Stecknadel fallen hören können.
"I'll tell you what happened that morning. Sylvie came to the reception desk early to talk to Alison Rutherford. She probably already had a gun with her, hidden away so that

---

unmistakably [ˌʌnmɪˈsteɪkəblɪ] unverkennbar **high-pitched** [ˌhaɪˈpɪtʃt] hoch **Let me get this straight.** [ˈlet mɪ get ðɪs ˈstreɪt] Lass mich das klarstellen. **to entertain** [ˌentəˈteɪn] unterhalten **to impersonate sb.** [ɪmˈpɜːsəneɪt] jmdn. imitieren

Mrs Rutherford wouldn't see it. Sylvie **distracted** Mrs Rutherford, maybe by **asking** her **for a light** or pretending she had forgotten her cigarettes. When Mrs Rutherford **was bending over** to look for cigarettes, Sylvie quickly wrapped up the weapon in a cloth to muffle the **gunshot** – and **pulled the trigger**." Laura strich sich durch das Haar und seufzte. Auch wenn sie wusste, dass sie das Rätsel gelöst hatte: Das Hochgefühl blieb aus. "And when Peter came into the lobby at seven o'clock to go jogging with Sylvie, he had no idea that Mrs Rutherford was already dead – she was hidden behind the reception desk. Later, Sylvie imitated her voice to convince Peter that she was still alive. And Sylvie probably threw the gun into the sea sometime later. She could be certain that nobody would ever find it."
Sylvie nickte lächelnd und seufzte aus tiefster Seele. "It's a **relief** that things are over. Alison wanted to ruin things for us, Clive. I thought if I could just get rid of her then our troubles would be over. I only needed to pull a trigger. It was surprisingly easy." Ihr Lächeln schwand. "But then David surprised me by coming down the stairs . . . "
Clive starrte sie entsetzt an. "David? Did you kill him, too?"
"Clive, I love you so much. I did it all for us."
Entsetzen stand in seinem Gesicht, und er wollte Dianes Hand greifen, doch sie drehte sich um und ging zu Fred Lightfoot.
"You **disgust** me, Sylvie!", stotterte Clive verwirrt.

---

to distract sb. [dɪ'strækt] jmdn. ablenken **to ask for a light** ['a:sk fər ə 'laɪt] um Feuer bitten **to bend over** [ˌbend 'əʊvə] sich herunterbeugen **gunshot** ['gʌnʃɒt] Schuss **to pull the trigger** [ˌpʊl ðə 'trɪgə] abdrücken **relief** [rɪ'li:f] Erleichterung **to disgust** [dɪs'gʌst] anwidern

Sylvie zitterte, und so sehr Laura sie verachtete, so sehr bedauerte sie Sylvie in diesem Augenblick.
"You haven't exactly got a clear conscience either, Clive, don't forget", erinnerte Laura ihn.
"But how did she kill David?", wollte Wolfgang von Laura wissen.
"She hit him on the head with that stone."
"Sylvie's stone", hörte sie Milena flüstern.
"Later she pretended that she had seen him in the kitchen and that he had made coffee. Really *she* had made it. She'd made it ahead of time. I could smell coffee from the kitchen before I got to the lobby. That puzzled me."
Sylvie blickte Beifall heischend um sich. "That's right. I followed him to the kitchen. David was standing with his back towards me, **fiddling around with** his mobile phone. I was afraid that he was calling the police. I had to do something fast. I grabbed the stone and walked up behind him. He didn't hear anything. I hit him on the back of the head. Then I **dragged** his body into the cold storage room. I'm stronger than I look. I do like to keep fit."
Sylvie kicherte und wippte mit dem Oberkörper leicht vor und zurück. Das ängstigte Laura noch mehr als alles, was sie in den letzten Tagen erlebt hatte.
Sylvie ist wahnsinnig. Wahnsinnig vor Liebe.
Es brach Laura das Herz, und sie schaute zu Peter. Er starrte mit dem gleichen Ausdruck von Fassungslosigkeit, Mitleid und Entsetzen zu Sylvie, die in diesem Moment weitersprach.

---

to fiddle around with sth. [ˌfɪdl əˈraʊnd wɪð] mit etw. herumfummeln **to drag** [dræg] schleppen

Übung 39: Setzen Sie die folgenden Infinitive ein.
*(believe, **incriminate**, create, point, think, **tighten**)*

"When I came back to check on Alison, I saw that she was wearing her pendant. I started to **1.** ______________ hard. I searched in Alison's book and found out that David was Taurus. So I took a Taurus pendant for him and hung it round his neck to make everybody **2.** ______________ that there was a psychopath at work. And even better", sie lächelte Diane wie in Trance an. "I hoped that the evidence would **3.** ______________ to her. It was great when Diane worked out the astrological sequence. That was more than I expected! And it seemed to **4.** ______________ the noose around her neck." Sylvie richtete sich auf und funkelte alle Anwesenden stolz an. "I knew that it was important to **5.** ______________ the impression that David was alive in the kitchen when I left. Then I could try to **6.** ______________ Diane by sending her into the kitchen alone later."

Sie kicherte wieder, erst leise, dann immer lauter.
She's losing it, dachte Laura.

---

to incriminate sb. [ɪn'krɪməneɪt] jmdn. belasten **to tighten** ['taɪtn] zusammenziehen **She's losing it.** [ʃiːz 'luːzɪŋ ɪt] Sie schnappt völlig über.

"That way Diane would seem suspicious. Yes, I was quite clever, wasn't I?"
Sylvies Kichern steigerte sich in Hysterie.
Laura nickte ruhig, und fast liebevoll sprach sie mit Sylvie. "You're very clever. But not clever enough. Poor Zaphira. She was your friend. Everyone knew she had brandy in her bottle. You kept brandy in your office, didn't you, Sylvie? Zaphira always wanted *you* to fill her bottle. Yesterday afternoon you took Zaphira into your room. You filled her flask with brandy ... But you put poison in there, too, didn't you!"
Sylvie nickte glücklich. "I learned a lot about **botany** from my Bridget. I've got some **deadly nightshade** growing in my garden. I doctored the brandy just like you doctored the soup, Clive. I gave it to Zaphira knowing she wouldn't be able to resist drinking the whole bottle." Sylvie lächelte Laura zu. "When she realized who you were, she got a guilty conscience and wanted to tell you everything. Now, I couldn't let her do that, could I? I had to kill her. But the poison caused her no pain. She had a wonderful death – peaceful and **painless**."
Fred Lightfoot, der wie die anderen schweigend gelauscht hatte, meldete sich plötzlich zu Wort. "But I thought she was strangled!"
Sylvie lachte selbstbewusst. "I only pretended she was strangled because that gave me another alibi!"
"You poisoned her long before, and when she was already dead you pretended to strangle her?", fragte Clive entsetzt.

---

botany [ˈbɒtənɪ] Pflanzenkunde **deadly nightshade** [ˌdedlɪ ˈnaɪtʃeɪd] Tollkirsche **painless** [ˈpeɪnləs] schmerzlos

"The police pathologist **would have discovered** that eventually", flüsterte Wolfgang.
Milena schlug mit der flachen Hand auf den Tisch. "Of course! That explains why the bottle didn't smell of brandy! Sylvie **had rinsed** it **out**!"
Laura nickte ihr zu. "Sylvie was very **resourceful**. It seemed perfectly reasonable for her to want to go and see Zaphira alone for a moment. None of us thought it was suspicious. She didn't have much time and she simply had a scarf **tucked away** somewhere ... "
Sylvie ergänzte seltsam fröhlich, was Laura begonnen hatte. "Up my **sleeve**. I tied it round her neck and **twisted** it tight. But she was already dead, of course. After cleaning the bottle to **remove** the last traces of poison, I screamed. It didn't take me more than twenty seconds." Sylvie sah sehr zufrieden mit sich selbst aus. "And don't forget, my dear, I put the pendant round her neck too. It was wonderful how **fate** caused them all to be born in such an astrologically significant sequence. It was meant to be ... "
Sie strahlte alle an, als hätte sie eine heilige Mission erfüllt. Dann zog sie stolz einen Brief unter ihrem Cape hervor. "And then dear Helga. I really didn't want to kill her, you know. I hope she survives. Why did Bridget have to write that stupid letter?" Wolfgang nahm den Brief vorsichtig an sich. Sie ließ es geschehen und lächelte ihn an. "Helga came to me with the letter. She adores me, you know. She would never do anything to hurt me."

---

to discover [dɪˈskʌvə] entdecken **to rinse out** [ˌrɪns ˈaʊt] abspülen **resourceful** [rɪˈzɔːsfl] einfallsreich **tucked away** [ˌtʌkt əˈweɪ] versteckt **sleeve** [sliːv] Ärmel **to twist** [twɪst] drehen **to remove** [rɪˈmuːv] entfernen **fate** [feɪt] Schicksal

Plötzlich und unerwartet sprang sie auf und schrie Laura an. "It's all your fault! You made her look for this letter. She **hunted high and low** until she found it. When she read it, she understood. She didn't care about Clive's reputation. But she knew if he went down, I would go down too. She didn't know what to do. She said that she had promised to give you the letter. I almost killed her ... " Sylvie sank wieder zurück auf den Stuhl.

"Shame she wasn't Cancer", kommentierte Milena trocken.

"And you changed her employment record and turned a Capricorn into a Cancer." Wolfgangs Stimme klang seltsam flach und gepresst. "To make the crime fit the astrological sequence. And that's where you made a mistake. I'm sure that you and Clive have different passwords. A computer expert will be able to **trace** who made the changes – you or Clive."

Sylvie hörte ihm nicht mehr zu. Sie lächelte Laura mit seltsam starren Augen an und redete sanft auf sie ein, wie eine Mutter auf ihre Tochter. "You look so much like your mother, Rhiannon. I loved her like a sister, you know. I can never forget her. She visits me in my dreams every night ..."

Laura fiel ihr eigener Traum ein, der Traum, in dem sie eine Klippe hinabstürzte.

"At night", fuhr Sylvie fort, "I can still see her swooping down into that black sea like a giant albatross. I can still hear her screaming, screaming, screaming ..."

Laura sank in sich zusammen, und die starken Arme Peters fingen sie auf. Die ganze Anspannung der letzten Stunden

---

to hunt high and low for sb. [hʌnt ˈhaɪ ən ˌləʊ fə] überall nach jmdm. suchen **to trace** [treɪs] zurückverfolgen wich von ihr; sie weinte leise. Wolfgang und Milena hockten sich zu ihr, während sie in Peters Schoß gebettet an ihre Mutter dachte, an ihren Traum und immer wieder an ihre Mutter, wie sie die Klippen hinabstürzte. An ihre Mutter, die sie niemals freiwillig allein gelassen hätte.

I promised I'd find out the truth, Mama.

I did.

Now rest in peace.

Dann wurde die Tür aufgestoßen.

Die Polizei war eingetroffen.

Übung 40: Welche Wörter gehören zusammen?

1. guilty	☐	**a.** killer
2. false	☐	**b.** silence
3. strictly	☐	**c.** alibi
4. astrological	☐	**d.** conscience
5. employment	☐	**e.** sequence
6. Christmas	☐	**f.** confidential
7. deadly	☐	**g.** record
8. serial	☐	**h.** tree

Epilogue

Sylvie wurde des mehrfachen Mordes angeklagt und für schuldig befunden. Clive wurde wegen Mittäterschaft, Falschaussage und Beihilfe zum Drogenhandel inhaftiert. Letzteres brach auch Ted das Genick. Helga eröffnete einen kleinen Massagesalon in Schweden. Jean-Paul ging mit ihr, und sie wurden ein glückliches Paar. Diane heiratete ein knappes Jahr später den Sohn eines Millionärs. Und Boun-

---

epilogue ['epɪlɒg] Nachwort

cer verbrachte noch viele glückliche Hundejahre auf einem Bauernhof.

In der Nacht, nachdem die Polizei erschienen war, hatte Wolfgang ein langes Gespräch allein mit Laura geführt.
"I was in love with your mother, too, as you might have guessed. We had one night together. That's all. It was long before she died. But I always felt guilty. Not knowing whether she might have committed **suicide** because ..." Er hielt einen Augenblick inne. "Bridget was never certain whether you were Martin's daughter or mine."
Laura hatte zuerst geschluckt. Wolfgang war also vielleicht ihr Vater?! Nur langsam und zaghaft freundete sie sich mit dem Gedanken an, einen zweiten Vater und in Milena eine neue 'Mutter' gefunden zu haben.
Peter und sie wurden ein Paar, und sie war – dem Grauen, das sie durchlebt hatte, zum Trotz – so glücklich wie nie zuvor in ihrem Leben. Zur Hochzeit überreichte Wolfgang Laura das alte Rezeptbuch ihrer Mutter. Clive hatte ihm verraten, wo Sylvie es versteckt gehalten hatte.
Die Insel und eine Hälfte des Spa wurden Laura zugesprochen, die andere Hälfte kaufte Wolfgang zu einem Spottpreis von Clive. Sie bauten das Spa komplett um und natürlich wurde als erstes der Pfad verändert, der 'killing arrow'.
Lauras Albträume kehrten nie mehr zurück.
Zwei Jahre später eröffneten Peter und Laura ein neues Hotel. Zu dem Zeitpunkt waren sowohl Laura als auch Milena bereits schwanger. Fred Lightfoot war ein gern gesehenes Original auf Rose Island. Er entpuppte sich nicht

---

suicide ['suːɪsaɪd] Selbstmord

nur als wunderbarer Gärtner, sondern gab auch Einführungskurse in Meditation für Erwachsene und Kinder. Er nannte sie 'Meditations in paradise'.
Von der Astrologie aber wollte niemand mehr etwas wissen.

Lösungen

Übung 1

1. ×, 2. ✓, 3. ×, 4. ×, 5. ✓, 6. ×, 7. ✓, 8. ✓

Übung 2

1b, 2e, 3c, 4g, 5h, 6f, 7a, 8d

Übung 3

1. went, 2. had, 3. saw, 4. took, 5. stuck, 6. knew, 7. bought, 8. paid, 9. kept, 10. came, 11. found, 12. was, 13. was, 14. became

Übung 4

1. knowledge, 2. cool, 3. close, 4. punishment, 5. easy-going, 6. unhappy, 7. hate, 8. lie

Übung 5

5, 2, 7, 3, 8, 1, 6, 4, 9

Übung 6

1. quickly, 2. immediately, 3. excited, 4. hardly, 5. perfectly, 6. normal, 7. fast, 8. steep, 9. eagerly, 10. terrible

Übung 7

1e, 2f, 3c, 4g, 5a, 6b, 7d, 8h

Übung 8

1a, 2a, 3b, 4b, 5b

Übung 9

1. remote, 2. opportunity, 3. including, 4. luxury, 5. according to, 6. mixture, 7. weight, 8. lose

Übung 10

1. The spa is now owned by former actress Sylvie Stone.
2. She is an attractive woman with red hair and green eyes.
3. She lost her voice and never acted again.
4. Cornwall used to be famous for its tin mines.
5. Fred Lightfoot is a bit of an oddball.
6. Cornish pasties are filled with meat and vegetables.

Übung 11

1j, 2c, 3a, 4f, 5g, 6d, 7i, 8e, 9b, 10h

Übung 12

1. more liberal, 2. further, 3. better-known, 4. more interesting, 5. more knowledgeable, 6. more sociable, 7. fussier, 8. worse, 9. better

Übung 13

1. dear, 2. hair, 3. blond, 4. became, 5. strange, 6. recipes, 7. hires, 8. herbal, 9. saved, 10. Soup

Übung 14

1. Sylvie recognized the perfume Laura was wearing because Bridget had also worn it.
2. They arrived at the island early because the current was strong.
3. Sylvie Stone and her husband Clive are the only two people who know the recipe.
4. Bridget Pencoe, Laura's mother, is the one who originally developed the recipe.
5. Dr Clive Stone was the last person to see Bridget Pencoe.

6. Yes. Sylvie tried to get in touch with Laura (Rhiannon) after Bridget disappeared, but nobody answered her letters.

Übung 15

1d, 2e, 3g, 4b, 5f, 6h, 7c, 8a

Übung 16

Results:
No Yes answers: You are a born sceptic.
1–3 Yes answers: You are curious about a lot of things.
4–6 Yes answers: You are a mystic.
7–9 Yes answers: **You are a firm believer** in astrology.
10 Yes answers: You are – or should be – a professional astrologer.

Übung 17

1. ×, 2. ✓, 3. ✓, 4. ×, 5. ×, 6. ✓, 7. ✓, 8. ×

Übung 18

1. mustn't, 2. used to, 3. can, 4. could, 5. shouldn't, 6. don't have to

Übung 19

1. eat/will lose, 2. Will Laura go/asks, 3. will be/manages to, 4. doesn't stop/will have, 5. will get/asks, 6. doesn't talk/won't find

Übung 20

1e, 2f, 3a, 4b, 5d, 6g, 7c

Übung 21

1. do you live, 2. am staying, 3. live, 4. am staying, 5. have just moved, 6. lived, 7. did you ever hear, 8. was

Übung 22

1. was trying/started, 2. met/was working, 3. were talking/stepped, 4. was living/met, 5. fell/were touring

Übung 23

1. shocked, 2. determined, 3. suspicious, 4. offended, 5. enjoyed, 6. pleased

Übung 24

1a, 2b, 3a, 4a, 5b

Übung 25

1. Milena said that Clive was the prime suspect.
2. Laura said that Clive and Diane were lovers.
3. Sylvie said that she didn't want to know.
4. Milena said that life was short.
5. Laura said that Sylvie believed that her husband Clive was taking her to Australia.
6. Laura said that Clive didn't love Sylvie any more.

Übung 26

1. shot, 2. muffle, 3. lighter, 4. jogging, 5. zodiac, 6. hear, 7. wet

Übung 27

1. ago, 2. at, 3. for, 4. in, 5. because, 6. while, 7. Since, 8. Although

Übung 28

1e, 2d, 3f, 4g, 5c, 6b, 7a

Übung 29
WATER: lake, ice, pool
EARTH: mountain, cliff, stone
FIRE: flame, lighter, sun
AIR: sky, wind, breeze

Übung 30
1. When, 2. until, 3. before, 4. After

Übung 31
1. angel, 2. Sweden, 3. improve, 4. sweets, 5. letter

Übung 32
1. praise, 2. thief, 3. argument, 4. ignore, 5. superstitious, 6. ladder

Übung 33
1. borrow, 2. eventually, 3. made, 4. wearing, 5. sensitive, 6. murders, 7. suspiciously/murderer, 8. mobile phone

Übung 34
1. suspicious, 2. package, 3. owns 4. expensive, 5. wages, 6. agreement, 7. in return, 8. persuaded, 9. bribed

Übung 35
1. Jean-Paul, 2. Sylvie Stone, 3. Sylvie Stone, 4. Sylvie Stone and Zaphira Parsons, 5. Peter Saunders, 6. David

Übung 36
1. ✗, 2. ✓, 3. ✓, 4. ✗, 5. ✓, 6. ✓, 7. ✗

Übung 37
1. ✗, 2. ✓, 3. ✓, 4. ✗, 5. ✓, 6. ✗

Übung 38

4, 5, 3, 1, 8, 7, 2, 6

Übung 39

1. think, 2. believe, 3. point, 4. tighten, 5. create, 6. incriminate

Übung 40

1d, 2c, 3f, 4e, 5g, 6h, 7b, 8a

Liebe Leserinnen und Leser,

Die einzelnen Titel aus der Reihe Lernschmöker sind den sechs verschiedenen Niveaustufen des Gemeinsamen Europäischen Referenzrahmens für Sprachen zugeordnet. Welcher Niveaustufe dieser Titel angehört, können Sie der Angabe auf dem Cover bzw. Buchrücken entnehmen.
Die Niveaustufen bedeuten:
A1/A2: *Elementare Sprachverwendung*, d.h.
A1: Sie können Einzelwörter und ganz einfache Sätze verstehen.
A2: Sie können ganz kurze und einfache Alltagstexte lesen.
B1/B2: *Selbständige Sprachverwendung*, d.h.
B1: Sie verstehen Texte, in denen v.a. sehr gebräuchliche Alltags- und Berufssprache vorkommt.
B2: Sie verstehen zeitgenössische literarische Prosatexte.
C1/C2: *Kompetente Sprachverwendung*, d.h.
C1: Sie verstehen Sachtexte, technische Fachartikel sowie literarische Texte
C2: Sie verstehen jede Art geschriebener Texte, auch wenn sie inhaltlich und sprachlich komplex sind.

Sollten Sie ganz genau wissen wollen, welche Niveaustufe für Sie geeignet ist, so finden Sie auf unserer Website unter www.langenscheidt.de sowohl eine kompakte Beschreibung der einzelnen Referenzniveaus als auch eine Orientierungshilfe zur Selbstbeurteilung in Bezug auf die verschiedenen Niveaustufen.
So finden Sie die Lektüre, die ideal auf Ihre Sprachkenntnisse und Bedürfnisse zugeschnitten ist.
Viel Spaß beim Lernschmökern!

Ihre Langenscheidt Redaktion